WORK LIKE A BOSS

A Kick-in-the-Pants Guide to Finding (and Using) Your Power at Work

Nancy Lyons

ISBN 13: 978-1-63489-354-1
Library of Congress Catalog Number: 2020909061
Printed in the United States of America
First Printing: 2020

24   23   22   21   20   5   4   3   2   1

Cover design by Luke Bird
Illustrations by Lisa Troutman
Interior design by Patrick Maloney

Wise Ink Creative Publishing
807 Broadway St. NE, Suite 46
Minneapolis, MN 55413
wiseink.com

For Merrick: Future. Boss.

CONTENTS

INTRODUCTION

In 2017 I was in front of several hundred people, delivering a keynote on leadership . . . and I found myself talking about menopause.

Five minutes before, I had been discussing workplace culture in front of this room full of professional women at the Business Women's Circle's annual conference. I was the opening keynote, so it was early and I was caffeinated. (The only way I'm a morning person is with a lot of coffee.) Even as an introvert, I love public speaking, and this was an exceptionally energetic crowd. I felt on my game. And then, out of the blue, my skin was glistening, my hair was frizzing, I could feel the whole hot-flash routine roll over me. You can't hide that. Even though it was a huge room, I knew they could see me sweating to death.

This wasn't the first time something like this had happened. I'm a woman of a certain age, as I like to say, and a big part of my life unfolds in front of people, whether it's on a stage at a conference, in an office during a client meeting, or in a boardroom as a director.

That day, I could have plowed on and tried to ignore my Texas-in-July body temperature and the glistening beads of sweat trailing down my cheeks in the name of professionalism. But I decided not to. I took a risk and said, "As I'm sure you've noticed, I am currently having the worst hot flash of my life."

And not only did the audience laugh—they celebrated. There was an instant buzz of energy in the room. Tension was released, and people saw themselves in that moment of humor and vulnerability.

Hi, I'm Nancy.

I'm the CEO of a tech company. I'm a gay woman. I'm a spouse. I'm a mother of an adopted son. I'm a loud prankster who needs to laugh to survive. I'm also a little heavy, I don't dress like a "lady," and I don't wear the right shoes or carry a purse. I have a big mouth and I was always a little too "direct" for traditional office culture.

This not-fitting-in taught me a lot over the years. In fact, I could say it led me to where I am now and to what I believe in most: we each have to create our own way at work. The power, joy, energy, and attitude we want to find at work are all derived from what we bring to it.

Our stories and experiences aren't determined by others. We can blame our manager, or that loud guy in the corner cubicle, or the woman who always shows up with the *best* PowerPoints. But that blame won't get us anywhere, and it certainly won't make us feel better.

Yeah, yeah, yeah, maybe you're a little distrusting of my work advice because I'm the CEO of my own company. I get to do what I want! I AM the boss! First, that is not the source of my joy at work ("thrilling" is not how I'd describe the day-to-day life of a CEO). Secondly, I am a CEO because I am basically unemployable (re: all the things above).

The thing is, in addition to being a CEO and a mom, I am also insecure, imperfect, still learning, and trying my best. I mess up sometimes, and I have emotional reactions to things that I really have no business reacting to in that way. I don't say everything the right way the first time around. I don't know everything, or maybe anything? Kidding. I know a few things. (Like every lyric to Duran Duran songs).

But that happiness I mentioned that you can find at work? It only happened for me when I started digging into and acknowledging all the things I didn't know or didn't do perfectly but tried to get better at. It came when I started to work openly with people and *for* people. When I started to get real with myself about who I was, what I wanted, and how to move in the right direction (however meandering the path ultimately was). And the solution wasn't starting my own company; it was being honest and vulnerable and truthful.

While I had to learn that the long and hard way, I hope to share some of my lessons and the stories I have heard on my journey so you have a shortcut to a little more joy and a little more empowerment at work.

A Little More about Me

There's literally being a boss, but then there is being a Boss, which comes before the actual job. Working like a Boss builds up skills and qualities that you'll need to be an effective and empathetic leader, regardless of your official position. Many people think that being a boss somehow bestows power at work, and in some ways it does. But waiting for the title or believing that you're powerless without the title doesn't help us. It diminishes us. Adopting Boss qualities taps into the energy, perspective, and attitude that we've been putting off and makes good use of them now.

I spent time waiting tables, which I think everyone should do to truly learn how to work with people and be patient. I did a stint in video production working for a really, really, *really* lousy boss (more on this later), and I know what it's like to be demeaned every day. I know what it's like to be devalued for what I look like and who I am. I was exhausted from being in places where I couldn't be my messy, honest, normal self.

Then one day I started working at a small, local ISP (google "ISP" if you are too young to know what that is) in Minneapolis. I met some guys who saw all of me—my drive, my buoyancy, my constant frizziness—and called it charisma. And after that company was successfully acquired, we launched a little company called Clockwork, and I got to be in charge.

I have run the sixty-plus-person agency for over eighteen years, and my spirit (a nice word for messiness) is welcomed. In addition to helping clients face big, janky problems, I steer innovation, manage critical relationships . . . and flip tables as needed. Yep, I finally am allowed to be my whirlwind self—my true self—at work.

Why Listen to Me?

Trust me, I ask myself that all the time. In fact, I routinely say to audiences, "Nothing gives me more right than anyone else in your life to say these things." I also point out, "I am saying nothing new. I'm just reminding you of things you forgot." I'm really talking myself up, eh?

But owning and running a company for as long as I have has taught me a few things.

First, I have to be honest about my background. Most founders would say they started their company because they had a rare vision, or they were so inspired by their idea that they couldn't devote their time to anything else. Me? I started my own company because I couldn't survive in highly dysfunctional environments—that is, most companies.

My experience with traditional companies, limited as it was, had showed me what I needed to know. I could see that people aren't often encouraged to help each other and are even passively encouraged to sabotage each other. The message, which is not said but is heard, is, "Well you *can* get ahead, but if you succeed they can't! (I mean, we can't *all* get up that corporate ladder!) So, in order to get ahead, you'll have to roll over that person next to you." And that was just the tip of the competitive iceberg.

I just couldn't survive in that environment. Yet that doesn't mean I don't still have access to it.

I have hired and led hundreds of people over the years. In doing so, I have witnessed the baggage that people bring to work and how that baggage influences them and the space around them. I have seen what personal characteristics help collaboration and what attitudes erode work culture. I have had long conversations with people from various backgrounds, with various work experiences, and in different positions. I listened hard and asked a lot of questions because I wanted to make our

company feel different than what I had personally experienced. It was basically years and years of user research.

I also see so much outside my company. By virtue of the work Clockwork does with clients, I see into their work cultures and their operations. (If you are one of my clients, don't worry: I'm not going to get specific!) I talk to CEOs, and I sit in meetings with cross-department colleagues and cross-functional teams. Digital work requires collaboration across silos, so I see and hear a lot about team dynamics and work cultures. Our human-centered approach, our design-thinking expertise, and our work in change enablement mean we ask tough questions about communications, operations, and processes. It's meaty, and it exposes a lot about what works at work and what doesn't. And client after client, project after project, we have learned that no amount of planning and talking can fix people who don't want to be fixed.

I see clear patterns.

- I see an inability to communicate, to the degree that it gets in the way of work.

- I see how people show up—or don't show up—when they aren't allowed to be their best selves.

- I see people throw literally *anyone* under the bus rather than admit that maybe they made a mistake.

- I see naysayers and negative chatter take over side conversations and then impact entire teams and relationships. ("Tom is such an idiot" or "Susan is always doing that . . . it's so annoying" without any communication with Tom or Susan. Poor Tom and Susan!)

- I see people trying so hard to be perfect that they end up flailing.

- I see how common it is for people to want to be told what to do, rather than figuring out how to do it.

At every single talk I do, people walk up to me afterward and tell me that it felt like I was talking about their workplaces. I hear from people *all the time* who tell me about the coworkers they don't trust, their go-nowhere jobs, the places they work at but don't care about, the fact that they are phoning it in, the fact that no one notices them working hard anyway.

All these experiences underscore why it's important to have the conversations we're about to have. To talk about how work feels, how we show up, who we blame for the problems, and what we do about those problems.

How to Use This Book

This book isn't linear. I want you to be able to pick it up, read a section that feels right for the moment you're in, and then set it back down. One day it might be the feedback section in chapter 6 because you know you're going to have a tough conversation with a client. The next day it might be the fear chapter because you're asking your boss for a raise or presenting in front of the executive team.

Work is hard. Humans are thinkers, feelers, and doers. At work, and through most of our intellectual upbringing, we're taught about thinking. But we have to fold feeling and doing into the fabric of work life to make it more compelling, rewarding, and reflective of our human experience. I hope this book starts to peel back the layers of the feeling and doing and how using those qualities can help you find a better work life.

I'm not here to teach you *how* to work, I'm here to remind you of things you've forgotten. It's going to be a lot of tough love. Not the shame-y kind. More like when your best friend tells you that you really shouldn't wear those pants ever again. Tough to hear, but coming from a good place.

All I want is for you to remember that you have the power to make things better. I am going to bring up a wide range of ideas and topics. That's the point. I have a feeling that when most people pick up a self-help book—even when they *choose* it—they create a distance between themselves and the content. "This is about people who are extra messed up! I'm just a little messed up." Until about page 10, when we realize that we *are* extra messed up . . . and all people are, really.

I deliberately include a menagerie of ideas because while the patterns of behavior at work are clear, where they come from and how they manifest vary, and what to do about them is nuanced and personal. You will see yourself in some things and not in others. You might see colleagues or friends in some of the stories. I don't go into depth on every idea. I want the book to be a catalyst for you to see yourself more honestly and then take steps to do something about it. On your own. Your power and joy are all yours, and *you* have to do the work to find them.

Don't think this book isn't about you. But also don't think this book has all the answers. Open yourself up to finding the answers and paths that are right for you through other efforts too. That's what a Boss is. They don't have the luxury of asking someone for the answer. They have to find it out.

Told ya, it's tough love time.

Chapter One
LIKE A BOSS

Before we get to what a Boss is and why you should put in the energy to work like one, let's talk about what it's like to not work like a Boss.

Work feels crappy and takes all your energy. You don't get along with anyone. You feel angry and resentful, and you bring negativity to work every day (or most days). You feel like nothing ever works out for you. You've kinda given up and become complacent. Maybe you participate in naysaying with your coworkers. Do you see yourself in some of this? No shame: it happens to all of us sometimes. And it has a bad effect on us.

But that's why you're here!

After spending hundreds upon hundreds of hours working with employees and clients, and talking to thousands of audience members at my talks, I started to see patterns. Patterns of apathy, frustration, and indifference. But also patterns of joy, discovery, and enthusiasm.

As I mentioned in the introduction, I am technically a boss, but so much of what I learned about how to work like a Boss came before that. It came through hard work and self-reflection during my time as a server, employee, production assistant, and salesperson. It came after tough conversations in which I had to admit failure or defeat. It came after observing others and being self-aware enough to see what really matters at work. It came from being dealt crushing blows by coworkers and colleagues alike and realizing how hard people can be on each other.

I was determined not to go through my life feeling like shit for forty hours a week. And I had to figure out how—but I knew bending myself to traditional "professionalism" or conforming to corporate norms wasn't a possibility. Like most people, I was highly influenced by my family, and I was lucky enough to have a mother who showed me a lot about how to be a smart, successful woman at work.

For all my mom's flaws, she showed very plainly how to do good work. I'm not just talking about work ethic, which she had, but also how to show up strong, confident, and human. She grew up as the youngest of eight kids in a working-class family: her dad was a bus driver and her mom was a cook at a construction company cafeteria. From there, she went to medical school at a time when very few women did, started her own practice, and built it into a successful business. The 1970s and 1980s in small-town Michigan weren't exactly the bull's-eye of gender progress, but she didn't care. She knew what she wanted, and she did it.

She was nonconforming, not just in the profession she chose, but also in how she literally showed up: she was 4'11" and probably 250 pounds. She was an overweight, unassuming woman who would walk through the hospital door and immediately seem ten feet tall. All because of how she showed up. She had Boss energy. I know because one of my first jobs was working for her. I saw how she ran her business and conducted her relationships. She treated everyone equally in a town that distinctly divided into haves and have-nots. She was absolutely direct in everything she said: she told it like it was without messing around. She knew medicine, and she knew people. I saw her do kind, generous things for people around her just because she could. And she always told me, no matter what, "Be educated and work hard." I saw every aspect of *Work Like a Boss* in her actions: her power was in how she behaved, not in her title, and she found joy in doing a good job every day.

I learned all that from her. Ironically, she encouraged *me* to conform even as she never did. I struggled, but I never lost what I learned from her at work. When I met my current business partners, I started to connect the dots on how work *could* be and how I could find satisfaction and power in the work itself. We were Gen-X poster children for the first evolution of change at work. We knew we were different than the boomers: we wanted to contribute to a shared purpose, and we wanted to control that purpose. I always felt like a misfit because I didn't behave right; in fact, we called our first company the "island of misfit toys." But we weren't misfits. We were on the cusp of a revolution in the workplace.

Right now, Millennials take a lot of crap because they want stuff that they "don't deserve" or "haven't worked for." When we were coming up, the way to "work for it" was to conform. You played by the rules for long enough and *then* you'd get an opportunity. What I saw in my partners was the opportunity I'd wanted from the start (and maybe hadn't "worked for"): to love work without conforming. Personally, I couldn't. And I also didn't think that conformity was actually good for business (but who would listen to someone with no MBA suggest how a business should work?).

Conformity implies that someone has done all the thinking and everything is set. Get in line, and do the things that are always done. But that's not actually true. There is always room for evolution and change. Innovation (or evolution) doesn't come with conformity; it comes with showing up differently, challenging the status quo, even irritating the conformers along the way. Whether you're an introvert or an extrovert, a thinker or a doer, an executive or starting out in your first job, a visual or a verbal processor, a Type A or Type All-over-the-place, you have a way of showing up and contributing. That's the capital-B Boss way. I wasn't positive I knew that I—or we—would find a new way to work, but I was positive that I had to try and that I would learn something along the way.

Working like a Boss has nothing to do with being a boss.

Breaking Down Bosses

So what is a Boss? According to the dictionary on my Apple computer, a boss is "a person in charge of a worker or organization or a person in control of a group or situation." A person in charge of a *situation*. That could be you. But it's not just about being in charge of people; working like a Boss is about being in charge of yourself, your surroundings, your sphere of influence, your reaction to things, and how you show up every day.

Here are a few bosses I can think of: Captain Kirk and, later, Captain Picard from *Star Trek*. Lou Grant from *The Mary Tyler Moore Show*. Meryl Streep in *The Devil Wears Prada*. The *Office Space* guy. Michael Scott from *The Office*. Steve Jobs. Elon Musk. Oprah Winfrey. Mark Zuckerberg. These aren't all good bosses, and that's on purpose. They represent what we all might think about when we hear the word *boss*. The bad ones have been as influential on our cultural understanding and practical experiences as the good ones.

The best bosses listen, are supportive, show up, have a vision, take initiative, can make decisions, truly care, fail well, are resilient, don't sweat the small stuff, are adaptable, are inspirational, are not afraid to try, don't get distracted by what other people think, show up willing to do the work, empower people, trust people, share credit with others—did I mention they really, really care? While all these examples are different, and some of them are pretty far out there, they all possess similar qualities, and no one can argue they all really care.

Bosses go into situations with agency. They don't assume a subordinate role within a conversation. They don't have to dominate, but they know they have agency and power because they are human and valuable, not because they have a title. This is a hard feeling for some women and people of color to embody because, well, patriarchy. But I've found that waiting for permission is time-consuming and boring. Bosses own what they can and slowly work on the rest of the power imbalances in the world along the way.

While these are all great boss attributes, they don't really have anything to do with leading people.

How I think about being a boss and how I show up at work goes directly back to my ten years in food service. To a time when I wasn't leading anyone.

When I took the time to smile and make eye contact and engage with customers, I made more money because they felt seen, heard, and appreciated. I didn't do this because I was their manager; I did it because I genuinely wanted to connect with my workmates and my customers. But it didn't take long to recognize that these behaviors produced the outcomes I wanted: it felt better for me, and I received larger tips (though that's a side effect). I noticed pretty quickly that when I didn't give a shit about my tables, they didn't care about me either—my energy and how I interacted with them shaped how they treated me. When I was having fun with my coworkers and my customers, my tables could *feel* that.

I guarantee you that I wasn't the best server, nor did I knock it out of the ballpark during every shift. But I learned that I had some control. Even when the actual boss was an idiot or we were out of everyone's favorite chicken dish or I spilled soda on someone's lap.

More than anything, working like a Boss boils down to being:

- accountable

- less fearful

- human and humble

- communicative

- caring

No big deal, right? Well, actually, yes. It is kind of a big deal. It's not always easy, but it is *attainable*.

There's no point in only doing the easy stuff.

Being the Boss You Are

So what's it going to take to inch—or leapfrog—your way toward working like a Boss? And why should you give it a shot?

Honesty

I remind myself every day that the easiest story to tell is the truth. Usually, I mean this literally: tell the truth when sharing information about a project, communicating about the company's goals, or explaining a mistake. But I also mean it poetically: tell the truth about ourselves, our strengths, our weaknesses, and what we want. But that honesty takes some work.

Honesty is hard because it requires a lot of emotional intelligence. We have to be self-aware and tuned in to others, *and* figure out how to navigate all of that. One of the things I've noticed after years of working so closely with people is that we (humans) aren't taught how to talk about emotional things. Hopefully, therapy culture is changing some of that, but then we also have to figure out the next step of bringing those skills to work, an environment in which we have historically kept our inner, personal selves separated from everyone and everything else. But there is hope. We can do this! (More about how in chapter 5.)

Throughout this book, I hope you stay honest with yourself about your own actions. Be honest about whatever positive or negative things are on your mind and whatever real intentions you have at work. It's important that you are truthful, at least with yourself. Otherwise, we'll get nowhere.

Being a human is messy, and no one stops being a human when we arrive at our jobs in the morning. And working is messy, and yet we all have to work. Working like a Boss means that you can see, take in, adjust, and deal with all the truths about you, others, and the messy stuff in between. It doesn't mean you'll do things right! It just means that you are honest about them all.

A Change Mindset

You're thinking about change *right now*, of course, but every company everywhere needs every person to have a change mindset at all times. Business is moving fast. Regardless of your industry or your role within the company, what you do and how you do it is changing faster now than it would have twenty years ago.

I frequently give a talk during which I spend the first ten minutes on a brief history of innovations and major developments that drastically impacted humans, such as fire and electricity. Humankind used to have decades or generations between major, life-shifting changes. We used to

have time to adapt. But internet technology basically went from zero to a thousand miles per hour within a single generation. Individuals who didn't have email while they were in college are now chief information officers. Think about that: something that wasn't even part of their daily lives is now their entire livelihood.

I work in the digital industry, so I hear a lot about "digital transformation." But the digital transformations we've made affect all businesses and industries, at all levels: logistics, transportation, service, finance, medicine, hospitality . . . the list goes on and on. I have no idea if the world will continue to evolve at this speed for the rest of eternity, but there is no sign it's slowing down for current generations. Technology has changed business, and people will have to manage this change. Enter: a change mindset.

Everything about being a Boss hinges on a change-oriented mindset:

- Accountability is about owning change.

- Fearing less is about getting used to change.

- Human and humble is about making space for change.

- Communication is interacting well with others during change.

- Caring about people and your work is essential to the process of change and also the foundation of successful change.

Being more comfortable with being uncomfortable is a mindset that we can all achieve. It's becoming familiar with yourself—your triggers, your motivations, your skills—and recovering every time you fail.

Unlearn Some Stuff

This book is as much unlearning as it is learning. Why? Because we have picked up some ineffective habits as we've grown up (like saying "I'm sorry" for everything, or replying to all on emails that really don't need everyone in the loop). And yes, I mean every single one of us. It's not our fault, per se. It's that our families of origin (the families or systems in which we grew up) and the institutions of school and work have molded us into people who aren't good at doing the things we need to do: communicate well, take risks and learn from mistakes, and partner with other people along the way to get stuff done.

In fact, some of the very universal lessons we are taught are *antisuccess* behaviors. I'm thinking of things like "behaving," not rocking the boat, deferring to authority, and assuming that there is a right way and a wrong way (and that, usually, the person with the most power knows the right way). Also that there is only *one* right way . . . there is one way to get an A, for example, and it's based on how every student before you has done it. We're taught (explicitly or implicitly) that some people matter more than others. And we're told untruths about how work works best.

Each of these things might be true sometimes, but not all the time, and they are definitely not useful for us in our day-to-day work environments. These lessons squash our sense of independence and power. They minimize how much control we think we have over our work and contributions.

It's like this stuff is in our cultural DNA or muscle memory. I think of my dad and the way he approached work. As a young person, he joined the army, went to the police academy, got married, went to college, graduated from college, got a job, bought a house, and saved a little for retirement. He put his head down and hoped to work at the same job until he was sixty-five. He didn't actually have the same job until he was sixty-five, but that was his definition of success. He didn't necessarily need fulfillment; he was just happy to go to work every day and get a paycheck. That's how so many baby boomers approached work and their careers. It was about outlasting it. *Surviving* it.

I think we all know things have changed. And yet, that mentality is still ingrained in different parts of our work culture.

Relearn Some Stuff

Much of what I'm going to say is basic. In fact, much of it is simple stuff you learned in grade school, but simple doesn't mean easy. If only, right?

Be nice to others. Share with others. Don't put marshmallows in your nose. These good lessons got complicated as we got older. "Be nice" turned into "If you don't have anything nice to say, don't say anything at all." Now, that's terrible advice. It should be "If you have something to say, find a kind way to say it." Not as catchy, but a heck of a lot more useful in life.

Kids run onto playgrounds and start playing with anyone who's doing something that looks fun. Our teachers told us to include everyone in our games and not fight. Playing well with others has matured into collaboration. In our grown-up, professional lives, this is known as compromising and adjusting. And just like on the playground, there will be fights and big laughs and hugs and sand in your shoes because, ultimately, real collaboration looks more like a marriage or an elementary school playground than anything else.

If we don't shift how we think about work, we will become obsolete.

Why, Oh Why, Do All This Work?

Because you have a choice. Because giving a shit feels better than not, and work is not fulfilling for most people right now. We are working our way *around* work: the surge in the gig economy demonstrates that working *for* someone or *with* people needs to be avoided. We won't last long if we keep that up.

Work doesn't have to be everything, but it should be *something*. But why? Why do we even care about how work feels? Who says work should feel good? And why does it matter? I think there are reasons that are even bigger than us, reasons beyond our own professional satisfaction and fulfillment. We know work is broken and big companies are messed up, but I honestly believe that if we don't start shifting how much we care and how we contribute at work, the United States will fall behind as a developed nation. We are already seeing the threat of other countries outperforming us. The cumulative effect of apathy, the same ol' same ol', cannot be good for us as a whole.

This book is an instruction manual—the perfect companion to your employee manual—for being a positive force at work (and, honestly, everywhere). It is a tool to help you recognize and call out counterproductive behaviors at work. It's a primer in things that will help you observe, change, and take charge.

No matter what your position, your energy affects your interactions with your colleagues, your clients, and yourself, and those interactions, in turn, affect the culture of your workplace. You can change the culture around you by changing what you bring to it.

Go from "meh" to meaningful connections.

Go from "I'll just do it myself" to being a better collaborator.

Go from "It's fine" to feeling good about work.

It's so tempting to abdicate responsibility for change to everyone (anyone!) around us—I'm as guilty of it as anyone. But think: isn't it nice when one person acknowledges your work, treats you like a full human, or collaborates on a creative project? It's elevating, isn't it?! So: be that person!

You are responsible for the energy you bring into a room. Your joy, your path, and your mindset are in your own hands—not your colleagues', your boss's, or your company's. You can break out of autopilot living to create a work-life *life* that is purposeful and exciting, and in turn, you give that revolutionary gift of new energy to the people around you. Even if you are far from the boss title, that's working like one.

Are you ready for this? I've been told that my directness, combined with how much I really care (which is a lot), makes a punch feel like a hug. That's what I hope you feel here: the punch of tough love in a package that feels like a hug.

Work Like a Boss Takeaways

1. Being a Boss doesn't mean being bossy or controlling. It is more nuanced and introspective than what we typically see out in the world, on TV, or in the business culture around us.
2. Taking ownership of how you show up—for yourself, others, and at work—is in your control.
3. Being accountable for how you show up can make work more meaningful, make work relationships more productive, and make you happier—all without changing anything else about your job.

Chapter Two

SHIT'S BROKEN

Remember that adage, "The first step to solving a problem is admitting you have one?" On behalf of the vast majority of workplaces in this country, let's admit it: Work is broken. It's slow to adapt, it's persistently biased, and it's hindered by a century of baggage. All this affects the humans in those workplaces.

What a pick-me-up, right? I promise this chapter will be more optimistic than that. In fact, I hope it will validate all the feelings you have about work and why you picked this book off the metaphorical shelf. (Let's be honest: you probably ordered the ebook online. Thanks, Amazon.)

Before we dive into how we can make work better—i.e., the rest of the book—I want to talk a little about how we got into this situation. Some of this is historical, and some of this is op-ed. I know I'm touching on something people *feel* but maybe have never been able to put their finger on because I see how people react to it when I finally say it out loud. I see people's eyes light up or teams exchange knowing glances around the conference table in that "Is she a fly on our wall?!" kind of way.

Work is a melting pot, maybe the only real melting pot we encounter.

In most parts of our daily lives, we can choose the people we're around. We choose our friends, neighborhoods, pastimes, places of worship, and hangouts. And because we're human, we typically choose people who are like us and environments that are familiar. But work? Nope. We might get to choose the company, and if we're a manager, maybe we can choose part of our team. But for the most part, when we're at work, we're surrounded by and interacting with people we didn't pick.

The melting-pot nature of work makes it fascinating, challenging, and unpredictable—compounded by the fact that we spend more time at work than any other single place, which means we're really in for a treat.

> *Workplaces aren't keeping up with the changing demands of the people doing the work.*

A Short, Relevant History of Work

Have you ever watched *Little House on the Prairie*? I read the books and watched the TV series, and I loved them both. But, for the purpose of illustration, let's talk about the show. When the series started, Ma and Pa lived on a farm with their kids. They were self-sufficient: Pa tended the farm, the kids went to school in a one-room schoolhouse, and Ma took care of the house. Then, much later in the series, Pa needed to make more money, so he moved to the booming metropolis of Mankato (Minnesotans will get the joke). His work maybe wasn't as fulfilling as farming, but as time went on, it was the only way he could make real money. The chasm between the haves and have-nots was growing, and this was the new industrial reality for Pa and everyone else. So, where once whole families were dispersed far and wide in rural areas, growing their own food, butchering their own meat, and living in single-room houses, suddenly many people (mostly the menfolk) were moving to urban areas for employment that paid enough to support their ever-growing families and their ever-growing needs at home until they could afford to relocate to the city. People were cogs in machines, valued only for how much they produced. (Sound familiar?) And there was a huge rift between the wealthy people who owned the factories and the poor folk who worked the factories. Pa was one of those working folk. And, miserable as he was, he was grateful for a job.

While the television version of *Little House on the Prairie* was fictionalized to some extent, it represents what was happening in the late nineteenth century: work as we know it was being defined. So most aspects of modern-day work came to be in a wildly different time and sociopolitical landscape.

The vast majority of our ideas about work were birthed sometime between the Industrial Revolution and post–World War II prosperity, everything from how we dress to how we interact to our expectations from ourselves and others. And guess who was making *every single one* of those decisions: wealthy, white, mostly straight men.

Along the twentieth-century way, the people in charge decided what professionalism looks like and how work works. Those people were rarely in charge because they were good leaders or because they cared deeply about the people they employed. They were in charge because they were men, they followed the rules, and they didn't mind making other people follow the rules.

Please know, I am not here to rail on men. I think everyone is a mess: men and women and nonbinary and everyone else. But it's critical that we acknowledge where our expectations—and baggage—come from. And the origins of our power structures.

What Work Used to Look Like

During the late nineteenth century and most of the twentieth century, work was transactional.

- The company had rules; people followed them.

- Companies had specific job descriptions; people showed up and performed specific tasks.

- Leaders supervised employees, and employees were evaluated by output. Everyone's value was wrapped up in either their production potential (employees) or the potential to make sure people were producing (managers).

When we industrialized, one could assume bosses—the people in power—didn't care much about the humans who worked for them. They put people in pens and worked them to the bone. That abuse was fought by unions and the labor movement, which gave us a forty-hour workweek and a minimum wage. But we are still left with the bulk of that biased, antiquated view of what is (and is not) professional.

As white-collar jobs became a thing, the people in power decided what professional looks like—and, along with excluding our best stuff, that flat-out doesn't look real. Professional lives are a mask we wear that accompanies the literal uniform of work clothes. This doctrine colors how we talk, how we take breaks, and how we do or do not address differences.

It also affected the developing role of human resources. Typically, policies protect the company and rules serve the organization and its objectives. Even in the most kind-hearted team, the rulebooks usually make work transactional.

The reality is that one picture of "business leaders" has been painted for decades, and that picture is largely white, largely male, and, for most of us, largely baby boomers. Guess what: that just ain't how the world is anymore. That's partly why work is so hard for so many of us. Business and work culture have evolved, but often workplaces have not. All is not lost, though! We can individually start to cope with and manage all this, even if the workplace around us is lagging. More on that later in the book.

Okay, the history lesson is over!

My First Hunch That Work Sucked

Many of my first bosses were terrible at being bosses. I have a boss story that's full of gender bias and passive-aggression—a delightful workplace sandwich!

Bad Boss was condescending and dismissive of my ability. For example, I had never worked on a Mac before (this was a very long time ago), and he would stand over me and watch me fumble around as I was learning the system. I remember him saying, "That took too long. Why would you do it that way? There is a better way to do it." I thought to myself, "There's a better way to be a boss too." But of course, I didn't *say* that.

It was the nineties, and because I've always been a bit of an early adopter, I got a cell phone. He said, "What do you need a mobile phone for? You don't do anything that important." Such a great person, right?!

He hired men vastly less qualified than me for higher titles. He hired women vastly more conventionally attractive than me and gave them hours of friendly (still sexist) attention.

So, basically, crap upon crap upon crap.

My boss believed that men had an inherent value and conventionally attractive women had a different inherent value—and that I didn't bring any value. That atmosphere contributed to how I showed up. Even when I was there physically, I wasn't *there*. This guy made me feel like shit, so shit was what I brought to work every day. And it wasn't only him: I was surrounded by people who subscribed to his treatment of me. Their actions compounded the feeling that I was less-than, and I became less-than.

The language of microaggressions didn't exist then, so I never named how or why Bad Boss made me feel like dirt. But I knew that he did.

It's not the natural order of things that fathers aren't legally obligated to get parental leave or that high heels indicate that a woman is taking a presentation more seriously. All the unwritten rules of work were compiled over a few decades by the people in power, who all, incidentally, looked and sounded very similar to each other, and to Bad Boss.

(Before you start yelling about me yelling about Straight White Men, let me say, I know lots of Straight White Men, and most of them are great people, as far as I can tell. Some of my best friends are Straight White Men. I actually grew up in a predominantly Straight White Men neighborhood.)

Now that we've got that out of the way, let's examine the unifying characteristics of the people in power in the late nineteenth and early to mid twentieth centuries, when the rules of work were being written. Funnily enough, they were almost exclusively men who were white and straight. Anyway.

Work Is Broken

I'm not going to name that crappy boss or even what industry he was in. It doesn't matter who he is as a person. All that matters is that he is not unique. He's not even the exception to the rule. *Still*, even with #MeToo and the internet and Millennials and Gen Zers pushing for change, there is a lot to fight.

We separate "home self" from "work self." We overvalue cognitive culture and undervalue emotional culture. We assume work must be serious. We focus on how to make the widgets better rather than how to treat humans better. I'm not going to lecture on how all this is connected to historical power imbalances, but a few Google rabbit holes can give you some insight.

On the company level, work is threaded with sexism, racism, homophobia, ableism, and ageism. There is a lack of concern for employee mental health. Many organizations (and boards of directors and leadership tables) are boys' clubs. There is not enough (or, frequently, any) parental leave. Little flexibility for family care. Little flexibility for cultural needs. Work isn't set up to merge with life at all. There are policies in place to help protect individuals from certain aspects of this brokenness, but policies can't correct culture. If internal attitudes or external pressures and stereotypes prevent people from taking advantage of the policies, then they aren't really policies. They are just ideas on paper.

On the team level, people are siloed into segments that don't know how to work together. The inevitable distance between management and staff perpetuates competition and power. Organizational charts, titles, and tenure dictate more about our compensation than how we contribute. We don't know how to communicate with people (don't worry, this is so broken that I devote an entire chapter to it). Our performance reviews are one-directional, not an open dialogue about how we're working (or not working) *together*.

One thing that I notice is our inability to talk about what we need at work. Both companies and people are stuck in an ineffective, looping dialogue focused on benefits, money, and perks rather than an exchange of value, contribution, and work culture. As more and more people work as freelancers or solopreneurs,[1] it appears that we're working around work.

---

1. Morgan Stanley, "The Gig Economy Goes Global," June 4, 2018, https://www.

Rather than fixing the crap we see and feel within salary jobs, people are going out on their own to foster and drive their own work experiences.

If you're reading this and thinking that one or all of these hurdles or opinions are overblown, then you are simply not the person affected by it. Take my word: when you're facing this stuff, it's big stuff.

In fact, I want to tell a story compiled from many conversations I've had with a friend who is a nurse in an ICU. When she talks about her work, it makes my skin crawl because it's so terrible and because it sounds like so many stories I've heard before.

She and I have talked extensively about why people enter the nursing profession: most feel a calling for it. Maybe an emergency happened and they recognized their ability to be helpful during periods of stress. Or maybe something happened to a family member and they wanted to help others in the way they were helped. Many professional origin stories start with the purest of reasons.

But then, a few years into hustling in the healthcare industry, they realize that A) they don't feel like they have a lot of power because most medical decisions are made by administrators and insurance companies, and B) there are very few positions that garner the level of respect that nurses deserve.

morganstanley.com/ideas/freelance-economy; Ben R. Matthews, "Freelance Statistics: The Freelance Economy in Numbers," August 29, 2019, https://freetrain.co/freelance-statistics/.

Nurses can move up the ladder into higher-level positions, but in order to secure one of those relatively rare jobs, they have to beat out everyone around them. What my friend describes is essentially an environment in which nurses mistreat rather than support each other. They sabotage how their peers are perceived by higher-ups. How they're valued or assessed isn't about their performance: they are valued based on the years that they've been in the job and whether they punch in and out on time. So their raise and promotion structures are not based on patient care: they're based on how many years you have been a nurse and if you've been late. I mean, it's not exactly that black and white. But it's close enough to be problematic.

What she describes sounds harsh, and I can only imagine the toll it takes on the people. Now, I'm sure not every hospital or doctor's office is like this. But some are. And I bet there are more than a dozen other industries that suffer from very similar issues. Here we see company-level and team-level brokenness trickle down to affect individuals.

How Is Work Broken? Let Us Count the Ways.

I don't want to dwell on the negative too much, but I'd like to bring up a few ways that work isn't working for us.

The Myth of the Personal versus the Professional

At some point in all the industrialization and corporatization of work, we drew a bunch of lines to distinguish what was considered "professional" and what was considered "personal."

Caring about numbers? Professional! Caring about people? Not between nine and five you don't. Talking about the presentation, the quarterly financials, or business development: professional. Talking about your stress, your family, or the stuff you're going through with your spouse? 100 percent personal, leave that at the door when you walk in.

Every day, I try to crack open the old "professionalism" framework because it doesn't really exist. We don't change into professional self at 9:00 a.m. and back into personal self at 5:00 p.m. All day, every day, we're both of those things. We're thinking about work or planning our career trajectory in the back of our minds while we're at the Little League game, and we're considering how we'll celebrate our kid's birthday while we're in a project planning meeting. And that's just the tasky stuff.

We carry emotional stuff between these two parts of our lives as well. One person can be both the fearful parent who is worried about being a terrible mom because she can't attend the kid's game *and* the fearful employee afraid to ask for an extra day to finish that deck for her boss. These fears bleed into each other and into all hours of the day. And that's okay—it's human. Anyone who thinks fears don't overflow into each other is very shortsighted or very effective at compartmentalization.

One of my favorite talks to give is called "There Is No Work/Life Balance, It's All Just Life." As you can guess from the title and my previous rant, I am always trying to dispel the myth that there is a difference between our professional and personal selves, or between our professional and personal lives.

Warning: that doesn't mean that you should share everything, all the time, with anyone at work who will listen. It just means that it's pointless (and impossible) to draw distinct lines between these two ways of being in the world and expect humans to stay on one side or the other.

I think it's actually detrimental to do that. Wherever I go, I try to create spaces where emotionally healthy values outweigh antiquated expectations. I know that people like working for me, and I think it's simply because I'm accessible. I want my team to see themselves in me because I see myself—my earnest, doofy, driven self—in every member of my team.

Too frequently, our cultural examples of leadership suggest that when you get there, you are no longer messy. I don't think that's true. Bosses are messy and flawed and fallible. They make mistakes, they fail, they lose sleep over embarrassments. And if they're good, they figure out how to combine honesty and dedication and move forward within that messiness. I want to work like that, and I want my team to work like that.

Swim Lanes, Hierarchy & Fiefdoms

I wish we could do away with all real and imagined hierarchy, but my friend and respected leader (hi, Meghan!) tells me that's not a good idea. People like structure, she says. People need structure, she says. I believe her, *and* I think we have internalized structure to mean more than it should for business today.

In theory, job titles and hierarchical layers can be helpful. Titles tell us, very generally, who does what. My title is CEO—that means I run a company. It also means I am responsible for the entire company. I have colleagues with titles like software engineer and senior UX architect. You wouldn't come to me with a question about coding or site architecture—you'd go to them.

Managerial layers exist to make things more efficient. If every CEO had every employee as a direct report, it would be untenable. It wouldn't make any sense for my software engineer colleague to come to me to work through complex questions about a coding problem she's trying to solve or even to evaluate her work. We have someone in place to do that. Again, in theory this makes a lot of sense.

In practice, though, titles and hierarchy also bring layers of unspoken baggage. Executives cling to status like it's their only identity. Managers cling to tiny bits of (perceived) power. And employees cower in their cubicles.

People care about titles and money more than they care about the work itself. Often, people ascend the corporate ladder based on tenure, not outcomes. Everyone assumes good ideas come from the top (or at least *should* come from the top). Messages and purpose get diluted as they trickle down through middle management. Employees end up feeling disconnected and confined to their job description, or confine *themselves* to their job description.

Really, every business needs everyone in a company, at all levels, to be thinking about fulfilling its purpose and delivering on its brand mission. We hear this on nearly every business podcast and read it in nearly every

Inc. magazine article about leadership. Yet those of us doing the work don't *feel* empowered.

You and I can't change all that BS about hierarchy and how people respond to it, but we can find ways to sidestep that baggage and productively work around it.

Work Culture Isn't Adjusting to Twenty-First Century Needs and Culture

Both of the above problems bubble up into this fact: workplaces aren't set up for how we—humans in the twenty-first century—want to be and work in the world. In *Drive: The Surprising Truth about What Motivates Us,* Daniel Pink shares the three things that motivate people at work: autonomy, mastery, and purpose.

We're living in a digital era without a chain of command: almost everyone has immediate access to people in power, and almost everyone has a voice (small though it seems on the social media landscape). Technology means that many people can work from anywhere.[2] Also, being in a chair from nine to five doesn't mean you're working hard,

---

2. This isn't true for everyone, I know, but each of us has more potential now to do some (if not all) of our work more flexibly—even if it's checking our weekly schedule from an app, sending an email to our boss at night, or placing that inventory order we forgot to send during the day from home.

while science has shown that really good ideas or breakthroughs can come when you're not working at all (as most of us have experienced).

Earlier in the chapter, I talked a little about work in early twentieth-century business as transactional (tl;dr: Jackie goes to work, clocks in, does a series of predictable tasks, goes home, and in two weeks gets a paycheck). Now, business is more relational: companies need to offer individuals more than just money, and individuals need to add value beyond punching in and doing the same five tasks they did yesterday. That's great, right?! We are no longer widgets! The world is growing up! But that also means we have to *act* like more than widgets.

Perhaps a good example of this new paradigm is the oh-so-trendy topic of Millennials. While Gen X broke down some of the "shoulds" established by the boomers and the Silent Generation before them, Millennials and Gen Zers are demanding different rules altogether.

Companies are spending millions trying to "figure out" Millennials while media headlines (and managers) rail against the generation's supposed entitlement and lack of work ethic. But here's what no one wants to admit: the only thing that makes Millennials different is that *they have the nerve to ask for the things we all want.*

A 2019 *New York Times* article asked, "Today's young workers have been called lazy and entitled. Could they, instead, be among the first to

understand the proper role of work in life—and end up remaking work for everyone else?"[3]

They're demanding to care about their work, not just do it for a paycheck (purpose!). They're demanding to work reasonable hours so they can also do other things they care about (autonomy!). They're demanding that business meet them where they are—technologically, physically, and psychologically. They want work to want *them*. In return, they want to give their employers more too. They're hyperconnected, they jump in with new ideas and explore new technology with ease, and they know more about business and entrepreneurship than any other generation because that's what the digital era (their era) is all about. It could be a win-win, if we just listened and adapted to some of these new ways of thinking about work. The *New York Times* went on to state, "Employees say that when they're not forced to cleave life from work, they work more, and more efficiently" (mastery!).

But despite these contributions, older generations resent Millennials for arriving with the expectation of a sustainable work life. They are criticized for expecting to be treated decently without toiling away for years and staying at work until 10:00 p.m. every night just to prove themselves.

---

3. Claire Cain Miller and Sanam Yar, "Young People Are Going to Save Us All from Office Life," *New York Times*, Sept. 19, 2019, https://www.nytimes.com/2019/09/17/style/generation-z-millennials-work-life-balance.html.

A survey conducted by Werk and quoted in the article above found that "Older employees are just as likely as younger people to want flexibility. They're less likely to have it, though, because they're less likely to ask for it. Sometimes, tensions flare between young people who demand a life outside work and deskbound older workers."

Well, that doesn't make sense. We all want it, but let's get mad at the people asking for it because . . . we only want it if *we* get it? Humans are so weird.

Millennials are asking questions that we should all be asking: How should work change to accommodate how we live now as individuals, families, and multigenerational households? How should work adapt to our needs so we can contribute more in the ways that work for us? How can companies infuse daily work with purpose to help work be more meaningful? How can work be more for us?

We're Broken

If you thought we'd get away with blaming every problem on work, you're wrong. We are very much a part of the problem. *We* means bosses, leaders, managers, employees. Humans. Every last one of us.

How we show up at work is entirely up to us. We don't remember this all the time, but it *is* true 100 percent of the time. No matter your boss, the company, your team, or your role, you determine the energy you bring to work. I'm not going to say, "All you have to do is think positively and your whole life will get better!" However, I am going to say that rather than acting as agents of their circumstances, most people act like work is happening to them. And once you think like that, there is no way to enjoy work.

We have to find a better way—for our own sakes.

The other day, I went to a sandwich shop after my son's baseball game. There was no one else in the shop when we walked in, and yet the one person behind the counter didn't greet us. We stood around for a bit and got a little uncomfortable that no one was even acknowledging us. Then I noticed a small sign at the opposite end of the counter that said, "Order here." We walked down, and the woman looked up but still said nothing to us. How do you think I felt at that moment? I felt dumb (because apparently we were waiting at the wrong end of the counter) and frustrated (why hadn't she just told us we were in the wrong place?) and confused (was I supposed to order from her now?). How do you think most customers feel going into that shop? Variations on dumb, frustrated, and confused, I would guess.

Now, I get it, she probably doesn't love her job. Her life probably isn't everything she wants it to be. But either way, she had to stand at the register that night and take our order. She could have chosen to be helpful. Yet she chose to be unhelpful.

After years of working with people in a range of jobs, in a range of positions, and across a range of moods (trust me), I can say without a doubt, it really does *feel* better to be friendly and it really does feel better to try. No matter how little else you have going for you at that moment, putting even a small piece of positive effort into something comes back to you.

It takes surprisingly little to make people happy. It's relationships and social connections. We can develop and foster these things on many levels: deep connections with our friends and family, but also simpler—though just as impactful—connections with colleagues, clients, and customers.

We Aren't Taught to Work, Nor Do We Learn

At school and in ongoing professional development, we learn knowledge and skills, but most of us don't spend time or energy on learning how to actually work with other people. Knowing your role is very different from knowing how to make your job effective.

The bulk of work comes down to interpersonal skills. We develop most of our interpersonal skills from our family of origin and hone them a little more as we go through school and college and get our first jobs.[4] Then we settle in. But remember what I said about work as the only real melting pot? These interpersonal skills collide in our day-to-day work life, sometimes wonderfully (think of the trend of calling close colleagues "work spouses"), but often poorly.

Consider this: we might learn how to improve our presentation skills, but you never hear of someone improving their skill in reading the room. Yet being able to gauge the temperature, mood, and energy within a room is just as useful a skill in the business world as speaking in front of an audience. That will tell you when to pivot, listen, or alleviate tension.

School doesn't always (or ever?) equip us with the tools to solve people problems. Frankly, there are more people problems than any other kind. Perhaps individuals consider "soft skills" here and there, but it's rarely a core focus in professional development or educational curriculum.

While it's not our fault that we aren't taught how to work, it is our responsibility to get better.

---

4. Team sports are another opportunity for people to learn about working with others, but I think what and how you learn on teams is limited and not always helpful at work. With sports, there is a rigid hierarchy that must remain intact no matter what. The coach calls the shots. So, while I don't dismiss the value of what is learned within group sports, it is distinct from the independent thinking and learning that happen elsewhere in our lives.

We're Social, We're Selfish, We're Social, We're Selfish

I want to share a thoughtful perspective from the founder of my son's Waldorf school curriculum, Rudolf Steiner. Although it is about school and was written more than one hundred years ago, it felt so applicable to our work lives today when I read it.

There are both social and antisocial forces working in each person, but our antisocial forces are getting stronger. Social forces make us want to do things for the greater good and to see the value in group success. Antisocial forces urge us toward separatism and ego saving. I'm not here to say one of these forces is more valuable than the other. I appreciate the tension and its power to keep things in balance. It helps us know when to come together and achieve as a group and when we might need to go at it alone.

In *The Social Mission of Waldorf Education: Independent, Privately Funded, and Accessible to All*, the author paraphrases Steiner: "He maintained that these antisocial forces, which are a by-product of the development of the human individuality, must be counterbalanced with ever stronger social forces, or else the antisocial element will gain the upper hand." Essentially, our antisocial (or ego-driven) urges are overtaking our social ones, and we're unbalanced. This reference dates to 1918, so I can't even imagine Steiner's horror if he dropped into our extreme world today.

In every situation at work, I try to focus my energy and the energy around me on the whole—rallying around what we're achieving together. When I can't stand the person I'm sitting next to or "that guy" on the project, I just remember the big picture: the thing we're trying to accomplish or the personal goal I can check off when I finish this part of my work. Just *something* that's part of the whole.

Negativity Bias Abounds

Holy crap, we are great at the negative things in life. We are great at thinking everything is going down the drain, we are great at noticing what's wrong, we are great at cataloging all the bad parts of our current job and few of the good.

Science agrees with this observation, which I've made over and over again as a CEO. Negativity bias is a real thing. The website Very Well Mind states, "Research has shown that across a wide array of psychological events, people tend to focus more on the negative as they try to make sense of the world. We pay more attention to negative events than positive ones. . . . We even tend to make decisions based on negative information more than positive data. It is the 'bad things' that grab our attention, stick to our memories, and, in many cases, influence the decisions that we make."[5] The article goes on to outline a study showing that human brains react to negative stimuli more powerfully than they do to positive stimuli, which has an impact on our memory, behaviors, and attitudes.

At some point in human development this was a very good thing. The negative stimuli—and our strong reaction to and memory of them—kept us alive. It was basic survival. But as our immediate environments have become safer, this instinct stuck around and now wreaks havoc on nonthreatening parts of our lives.

At work, this negativity bias influences a lot. According to research done by Teresa M. Amabile, a professor of business administration and director of research at the Harvard Business School, a negative setback

---

5. Kendra Cherry, "What Is the Negativity Bias?" Very Well Mind, April 11, 2019, https://www.verywellmind.com/negative-bias-4589618.

at work affected people twice as much as a positive step forward. She notes, "The power of a setback to increase frustration is over three times as strong as the power of progress to decrease frustration."[6]

Negativity—and its gravitational pull on us—is a theme I will revisit throughout the book because I've revisited it throughout my professional life, both personally and as a leader. Negativity gets in the way of so many people and prevents them from having a more productive and proactive response to the world around them. To me, the opposite of negativity isn't positivity, it's complacency. It's the energy equivalent of the shrug emoji.

It's Hardly Ever Us That's the Problem

I'm not sure where our aversion to being wrong stems from, but it's rampant. We are too proud or too embarrassed or too stubborn to say, "Maybe I'm part of the problem," or, "Maybe I can do something about this problem." We look to others to take the reins: the company, the leadership, our bosses, our colleagues. Literally anyone other than us.

---

6. Alina Tugend, "Praise Is Fleeting, but Brickbats We Recall," *New York Times*, March 23, 2012, https://www.nytimes.com/2012/03/24/your-money/why-people-remember-negative-events-more-than-positive-ones.html. Honestly, read this whole article! It's a quick and easy read that touches on personal and professional impacts of our negativity bias and some of the root causes.

Throughout my years of hiring and promoting people, one of the traits I looked for most was a focus on solutions. It's not catchy and pithy, but it is a sign that a person isn't looking to find fault or point to others as the problem. It always showed me that they were more concerned with making things better than slicing the blame pie.

The thing is, no matter what the original problem is, we become the newer and bigger problem if we don't try to fix things.

The Stories We Tell Ourselves

When we look at the monolith of capital-W Work, we find many things that we as individuals believe perpetuate its brokenness. We tell ourselves stories like:

"This is the way it's always been, so it will always be like this."

"I'm just one person, I can't change anything."

"I will get fired if I rock the boat."

We tell ourselves stories about why it's not worth changing, so we keep on keepin' on. But those are just stories. If we allow it, they will dictate too much about how we act. I don't have to look far to see the damage that negative stories can have on someone's outlook about work.

For a while, my father was the chief of campus safety in the small town where I grew up. In a handshake deal with a friend, he left that job for one at a private company as their director of corporate security.

It turned out that people at the new company were doing questionable things (maybe illegal, but definitely not what they were supposed to be doing). When my father tried to bring it up, the leaders didn't want to hear it and fired him. This single crappy experience framed his view on work and work culture forever. The lessons he took away were mostly about keeping your head down and doing your work no matter what's happening around you; if you have a job, you should do anything to keep it, no matter what.

While I empathize with my dad and feel bad about how that experience affected him, I entirely disagree with the conclusions he drew and the mindset he adopted. I think he let the power of his stories overrule the truth: that was a single crappy place to work, but not representative of all workplaces.

We have the power to change our brains. We have the power to do things differently if we tell ourselves different stories: whole-focused, positive stories that focus on the purpose—our purpose—at work. If work sucks, it's because we let it suck. Because *you* let it suck.

Work Like a Boss Takeaways

1. Work is still adjusting to what people need and expect from their professional life in the twenty-first century.
2. How we talk about and understand work has to evolve.
3. Our own habits and education (or lack thereof) prevent us from seeing ourselves as part of the solution. Yet we are central to the solution.

Chapter Three

OWN YOUR SHIT

In the next five chapters, you'll hear advice and lessons I've learned from personal experience and from talking to other people about theirs. Working like a Boss means embracing the straight talk that most people need to hear but no one wants to say (that's the kick-in-the-pants part). So here goes.

The other day I came across a clip of Lizzo performing at one of her concerts. I was mesmerized. In classic Lizzo form, she was sharing thoughts and encouragement with the audience and said, "The world is full of problems, but we can fix them if we start with ourselves." Fans erupted with excitement, singing, jumping, and dancing. The crowd pulsed with energy and enthusiasm—lighters swayed and people cheered.

I was amazed. They were joyfully embracing the idea that to make change out in the world, they had to start with themselves. And for a brief, Lizzo-induced moment, they saw themselves as part of the solution.

If I could get people to be that excited about starting with *themselves* to drive change *at work*, I'd die happy. People are so eager about self-improvement in other areas, like love, friendship, or family, but they throw their hands up in the air when it comes to work, thinking, "That's my boss's job," or, "I just work here." We act like, somewhere out there, there is a fantastic workplace that isn't like all the other places we've seen or heard about.

Someone once asked me to describe the ideal workplace, and here's my truthful answer: I don't think there is any such thing.

Every person is different, so every small role within a larger organization requires different support structures, and I'm not one for cheesy generalizations.

Also (and if you work in HR, stay with me here), work mostly *sucks*. Even when it's fantastic, I'd still rather be on a beach. And oftentimes, it's not fantastic.

Like most things in modern life—including relationships, family, and happiness—we romanticize work. We talk about work as if there could be a 100-percent perfect, every-day-is-heaven job that we are (or could be, or should be) headed toward. We toss around sayings like "When you find work you love, you'll never work a day in your life." We look at inspiring posts on Instagram about living your best life in your dream job. We say "When I get a raise" or "When I get a promotion" as if things will dramatically change.

But that's not how things (or jobs) work.

By all means, I'm not saying you will only ever hate your job. In fact, I think that getting real about the occasional-to-frequent suckiness of work is the first step to owning as much power as possible in your job. The reality is simply that jobs will always suck at least a little because jobs function within groups of people, and wherever you put a bunch of people, there will be problems. Interpersonal, institutional—you name it, work's got it.

Here's the thing: owning your shit is hard. Owning the problem *and* the solution takes work. Work will never be ideal, but our mindset can be.

There is no truth to find outside yourself.

There Is No Ideal Work, Only an Ideal Mindset

We have a pretty great little company in Clockwork. I'd never say it's perfect, but we work very hard to offer a decent, comfortable, and authentic place to spend our working lives. And I always notice that after working at Clockwork for a year or so, employees start to criticize it and take some of our work culture benefits for granted. It's the "grass is always greener" or "bright shiny object" syndrome. The honeymoon period wears off, and the competition starts to look mighty nice. "I bet

that other company doesn't have an annoying policy about this or that." (Spoiler: they do, or something just as irritating.) We get insulated and stop seeing the really great things around us. It happens to everyone about everything: relationships, that new car, a new gadget, and our work.

Maybe the grass *is* greener at some companies. But the grass could also be greener where you are if you help fertilize it. It doesn't matter how hard you focus on the ideal job or workplace or how hard you search for the perfect fit; what matters is the person you are at work, whether in an average role or at an "ideal" company.

Laboring under the delusion that some specific position or boss or company will make us feel whole and valued doesn't get us any closer to that fantasy world, but it usually reflects negatively on the job we have now. Remember that negativity bias we're all likely to have? We're much more apt to notice the bad things than the good things. We have to continually counter that.

I speak from experience when I say our mindsets need constant attention. Some days my mindset is in a crappy place: I am annoyed that a problem isn't getting solved or frustrated that we don't seem to be making progress on something that I care about, or I feel stupid because I misunderstood something. Moments like these happen to all of us because we are all humans with a job. But I can't walk into the office or get on a call with my colleagues and operate from those mindsets. It's not fair, it's not productive, and it won't help anyone (even myself).

Other than figuring out how to simply not work, the way out of a crappy mindset isn't searching for a new company; it's searching for a way to overcome that state of mind and be productive and effective.

At our monthly Clockwork staff meetings, I often say, "I can't make work not suck. You will have tight deadlines. You will face problems that feel unsolvable. And you will find yourself in conversations that make you want to cry, or yell, or both. And I won't be able to do anything about that, even as your boss. But I can say this: I care. I will continue to care. But I can't make work not feel like work."

Caring is all any of us can do. Care for some aspect of our work, care for our own mental health, or care for the people around us. Deciding to give a rip can be magical.

Finding that thing to care about is on you. Maybe you care because you want to eventually get promoted. Maybe you care because you really respect your colleagues. Maybe you care because you want to do a good job, regardless of what it is. Maybe you really like one of your clients or customers. Finding a connection that taps into your emotion and soul is necessary to feel accountable.

So it's on you—*yes, you, Taylor or Jo or whatever your name is*—to make your job better right now.

MINDSET

Fulfill Purpose — Feel Invested

There is no right way or one way to find fulfillment at work. We each have to find our way.

Ownership 101: Accountability

I have wished for other people to fix workplace culture before, rather than taking it upon myself to change. And guess what happened?

Nothing.

Sometimes I was hoping an organization would spontaneously enter metamorphosis. (Fat chance.) Sometimes I was hoping my boss or that annoying colleague would become the most perfect versions of themselves. And sometimes I was hoping to walk into a radically new office on Monday morning without lifting a finger myself.

But nothing changed when I didn't change. When you think to yourself (or say to your work spouse), "This place sucks," do yourself a favor and pause. Give yourself the opportunity to turn that around and own the moment. A workplace is made up of thousands of tiny employee decisions, thoughts, and interactions all day long. It's seductive to assume that an organization will (or even can) do the heavy lifting, but if members of a community don't take the evolution upon themselves, a transformation strategy is nothing but a paperweight.

The solution: stop looking at leadership to do it. Stop looking to hierarchies to tell you what to change and how to grow. You are accountable. It might not be on the accountability chart or the org chart or in your job description—but that's the problem. Most of us look at what we're supposed to do "on paper" and stop there. Yet that's what's slowly driving us into sad, dissatisfied work corners. We do want more—like purpose and a sense of being invested. You can make that happen all on your own.

I like saying, "Show up or shut up." Show up with the energy and commitment you want to see from leadership or whoever you're looking to for permission. Show up for the company and for your role with the purpose and passion you think might be at that other "ideal" company.

I know this is much easier said than done. Maybe you're already thinking about one of these counterarguments:

- I am just one person; how much can I really do? (More on that below!)

- It's easier not to change. I don't have enough skin in the game to care.

Here's the deal: if you don't care, I can't make you care. But I can tell you that rolling your eyes at work from morning to afternoon is a crappy way to live. Stepping up to the plate affords you some degree of personal power, regardless of how much external power you have and whether that matches how much you deserve. Pay attention to the power you do have and channel that.

And if you want other people to fix their shit, do the hard work and fix your own shit. You'll be amazed at the ripple effects.

Creating a Self-Culture Can Change the Microculture

Work culture is finally getting attention from companies—big and small—but it's a difficult thing to talk about. We often talk about the wrong things. We focus on the perks or benefits as the ingredients of a work culture, but it's so much bigger and more ambiguous than that.

When my cofounders and I started Clockwork, it was clear that the most critical element of our plan would be the people. Way beyond hiring people who could do their jobs, we focused on finding people who would work hard to foster, protect, and shepherd the culture that we four founders seeded. And that culture is entirely centered around values. We didn't want people who were all the same, but they had to believe in some of the same things. We had to value the same things. That creates safety and common ground even when all other factors (like personality) run the gamut of possibilities.

We had an employee leave Clockwork, only to rejoin the team about a year later. He told me, "I just realized that shit's the same everywhere, so I want to be in a place where I at least like the people. Work is work, the people are the main difference." Because people make up the culture!

Values drive culture. Your personal values will drive your self-culture, which will impact the microculture around you—like your team or a client relationship. You have this power, right now.

Before Clockwork was even an idea, I worked at Chi-Chi's ("A celebration of food!"). It was a huge chain at the time, so everything about the organization existed in a manual. There were many locations, and each was expected to operate the same way: employees wore the same uniforms, kitchens served the same food, and dining rooms looked nearly identical. Typical chain restaurant. But the culture at each location was different because of the people who worked in each store. I was in my twenties when I worked there, and I am *still* friends with my coworkers.

Did I love slinging chips each night? No. Did I love the two hundred times customers asked for more free salsa? No. Did I love showing up to work with the people who would become some of my best friends in my whole life? Hell yes. We loved coming to work.

We contributed to a culture—a microculture—that we brought to work each day. It was fun, and I knew they had my back. We'd walk each other to the bus; we'd go out after our shifts, and whoever made the most tips would buy. We cared about each other. We all grew up and went on to build careers in different businesses and industries. I'm an owner of a tech company, one of them is an organic farmer, one is a professor, and one is an attorney for the federal government. But we still carry some of those very early, very valuable lessons with us every single day.

If you ask what came first at Chi-Chi's, the culture or the friendships, it was the culture. We contributed to a common energy and common experience, and through that, we became close. That's the result of owning your culture: real connections, real care.

Your personal values will drive how you show up for yourself, for others, and for the organizations in which you work. They will help guide you when you're frustrated, when you fail or succeed, and when you're celebrating. They will help you navigate difficult moments and strategic decisions. They will also help you be consistent when so many parts of ourselves and our work change. Values are the things you can care about when nothing else seems worth your care.

For the first half of my career, I was in the closet. I thought that being honest about my identity would take away from our business. I thought if I were out and open, clients would avoid us and great talent would go elsewhere. It was only after deciding to be intentional about the life I wanted to live that I realized being in the closet was not in line with my personal values. How could I expect my colleagues to show up authentically with a willingness to take risks if I wasn't?

I often tell people that the day I decided to live my truth was the day I said yes to success. Shifting how I was in the world, being proud and honest, opened up new energy and new opportunities. Instead of dissuading clients and talent, we attracted people who were appreciative of our openness. So much so that in 2012, when the state of Minnesota put the issue of gay marriage on the ballot for citizens to decide whether it should be legal or not, our little company played a small role in changing hearts and minds. The entire campaign relied on the stories of real humans, sharing experiences that, instead of separating us from or making us different from our neighbors, really united us. Because really, all humans want the same things: to be safe, seen, heard, and loved.

Because of our culture of inclusivity and truth, Clockwork was one of the few businesses that participated in the campaign with no fear. We were loud and clear about the importance of *all* people in the Minnesota talent pool. If the state voted in favor of equality, we would attract more qualified talent for our workplaces. And that's exactly what happened. To this day, I'm proud of the tiny role that Clockwork played in this important story. And I realize that none of that would have happened if I hadn't started with myself. I had to own my own shit in order to show up for the greater good. I didn't know it at the time. But wow, am I grateful in retrospect.

Defining Your Values

Values aren't something most organizations or individuals plan out. Companies write business plans with financial projections and year-over-year headcounts. People plan what profession they go into and do a ton of editing and reediting of their resumes and LinkedIn profiles. But no one, outside of corporate marketing departments, actively talks about values.

Culture—in a workplace or within yourself—isn't just declared once. It's lived. It isn't static; it evolves. And keeping culture healthy requires vigilance, commitment, and self-awareness. The same is true for your self-culture.

Values don't have to be *about* work. At Clockwork we have five values: we tell the truth and keep our promises; we are helpful, curious, adaptable; and we are fueled by challenge. Those things could be applied outside of work too. If your personal values are true, they will be true in all areas of your life, not just work. That's what makes them so authentic and powerful.

Try making a list of the qualities and behaviors that matter most to you; a list that defines how you show up in the world. Now, refine your list to five things that you want to be your core values. These are what you will use to define and guide your self-culture: the energy you bring to people, situations, and problems. You might have to come back to this over time. That's okay! Owning your shit isn't something you do once for thirty minutes and then check off the list. It's a process and an evolution.

Once you have identified some values, it's your job to apply them to your life. Find ways to embed them around you or ask someone you trust to be a watchdog for you—tell them your values and give them total permission to point out when you might be straying.

Change is not about where you are; it's about *who* you are. Consider a bad romantic partner: if someone doesn't deal with their communication issues or fear of intimacy, every relationship will suck because they made it suck. Work is a giant tapestry of relationships, so be someone you would want to be in a relationship with.

*The most important thing is **to do**.*

Own It in Full: Moving from Mindsets to Behavior

As much as I talk about the power of your mindset, it can't stop there. If you're feeling truly accountable for work, you want to *do* something. You want to work more like a Boss!

If you remember nothing else after reading every page of this book (which you obviously will), remember this: *action is everything*. I am not suggesting that you have to do everything all at once. I am suggesting that you take *some* steps in a direction that you *think* is the right one, given the information you have at this moment.

Bosses have to move. They take action; they find the headspace to tap into the rational, action-oriented side of their brains.

I've noticed that the people who are already working like Bosses have some similarities, but they aren't the same. Bosses can be introverted or extroverted; college educated or not; can identify as woman, man, or a different gender; dress up or dress down; be tech-savvy or not. None of those superficial things define how we show up at work.

So here's my list of how to own an hour, a day, or your entire role at work. Not every action will resonate with you, and you won't always be perfect at the ones you take. Some days you will have to dig deep down to try even one, and other days they will come to you with ease. As I've said, working like a Boss isn't a destination, it's a way of being. It's a big work in progress.

Be Vulnerable and Have Humility

Our culture doesn't create a lot of space for leaders to mess up, yet one of the most important things Bosses do is create space for themselves and others to fail.

Most entrepreneurs and successful business owners would agree with me. I am in a peer group of women presidents of companies that range in size up to $100 million. And I will tell you this: every CEO I've ever met is entirely flawed and human, has failed many times, and doesn't know everything (and they'd never tell you they do).

The day we accept that about *ourselves* is the day we stop subjecting ourselves to the pressure of being perfect. And start *doing* without fear of doing it wrong.

I am so keenly aware of how flawed I am that I prep people for it. When someone at Clockwork was going through the gender transition process, they came to talk to me about how to plan for it at work. I was super frank. I said, "I am going to make mistakes. I am going to accidentally use the wrong pronoun. It doesn't mean I don't respect you as a human or your identity. But I am human and will mess up, even with the best of intentions." It is on me to do my best—you can't just say, "I am going to mess up" as an excuse to not try—but my best will never be perfect. And, reader, I did screw up. When I did, I apologized and corrected myself. But feelings weren't hurt because they knew my intention was respectful despite my mistake.

I knew I was on to something when I was mentioned on the radio. (And not in the way you think.) In 2018 Kerri Miller, a radio host at Minnesota Public Radio, was interviewing a group of local women entrepreneurs. She asked them who they admired: one said Beyoncé, one said Oprah, and one said me. The host, who I happen to know, said, "What I really appreciate about Nancy is that if she doesn't know something, she will say she doesn't." Have we reached a point in our culture in which I get a shout-out because I say, "I don't know"? I hope so!

I have nothing figured out. But I know that when I'm vulnerable and humble, I feel more powerful. I talk about my baggage because it's part of my story. What I don't know is part of my story. My ADHD is part of my story. My failures are part of my story. If I don't acknowledge all of this, then I (along with everyone else) am spending time and energy working around it rather *with* it.

BE VULNERABLE

Vulnerability and humility are some of

our greatest tools. Have tolerance for flaws and errors. Accept them in yourself, and support others in accepting theirs.

Add Value Where You Can

Maybe it sounds flippant to say "add value," but *you know what your organization needs.* Every organization, team, or department has room for improvement. I doubt anyone would disagree with that. But, like I've been saying, we can't expect anyone else to take care of all those improvements. No single boss or leadership team has the time to perfect every detail of work for every human at the office. Adding value means looking beyond the standard to-do list and seeing how you can improve the quality of the business, even a little.

Start with what *you* wish would change and fix what you can, step by step. Less complaining, griping, and wishing things could get better. More ideas, solutions, and suggestions. Is it stricter meeting limits? More cheerful interpersonal interactions? Fairer reporting structures? No matter what your position, you can take baby steps toward influencing any element of your workplace. Even a complex topic like reporting structures can be unpacked if you approach it creatively.

Have you ever noticed how easy it is to point out what's broken? We've all seen others do it and been annoyed. It feels like when a child says, "It's not fair." Yep, thanks for pointing out the obvious! But what are you going to do about it? That's what counts.

ADD VALUE

It can be really hard to initiate possible solutions. When we do it, we're not only coming up with new ideas but also working against our negativity bias! Each time we try, we are reprogramming our brains to react differently than they've been reacting for a long time. A first step may be moving from "No, but" to "Yes, and." Yes, brain, the weekly planning meeting sucks, *and* if we make the meeting shorter, we might see if timeboxing helps us stay on track. While we don't have biology on our side, we can do this!

The "Yes, and" trick is referenced a lot in leadership training and has roots in improv comedy. I was a theater major in college, so I learned that technique when I was young and have been applying it to work situations for years. It's a core principle because it opens up a dialogue rather than closing it down—and in improv, that's required. But this energy of opening things up is useful in so many other areas of our lives, including at work. It's a way of being that is genuinely helpful and alters your own attitude when you really own it.

Open Your Mind and Your Eyes

I've found that curiosity and observation are powerful tools in business. Smart people don't magically know everything before walking into a conversation or a meeting. They didn't have ideas or answers before immersing themselves in learning the work. Their Bossness came over time as they connected dots.

Watch the conversations that happen around you and see what you can learn about how individuals present their ideas. If someone appears to have it all figured out (spoiler: they don't), watch how they hold themselves and interact with colleagues. If you have a friend who loves their job, talk to them about how they show up. How do they overcome obstacles? How do they react to colleagues who annoy them? How do they talk to higher-ups? What is their mindset when they go into a hard

conversation with a client or customer? Taking inventory of how others "perform" work can be illuminating. It's how I learned much of what I know. Plus, most people love talking about themselves: capitalize on that!

After watching and inquiring, don't mimic the people around you, but instead find ways to improvise and test out new ways of working for yourself. Any successful person will tell you that there is always some "fake it 'til you make it" at work. We'd be nowhere without the white lies of "Yep I can do that!" while casually googling how to do it. Or, if you're in customer service, try being really positive for one hour and see if it feels different. People treat you differently when you treat them differently. (There will always be a few jerks who don't, but they are fodder for stories to share later with friends.) Don't take how people treat you personally—that's on them. But how *you* treat others is on you.

I have to share some bad news: this will take time. But don't give up! Whether you're successful in making your immediate work situation better *right now,* in two weeks, or, sadly, never, the reflexes and skills you gain along the way will pay off. You're in this for the long haul, so be strategic with your energy and ideas.

Take Initiative

No manager or business owner will turn down a good idea. They might take credit for it (which sucks) or change it a bit, but that just shows you that it was, in fact, a good idea.

Don't be afraid to test something out to see how it works. If it does, then you have data to bring back to your manager or team. Try saying, "This is new to me, but I got this." Even if it's just to yourself. You are acknowledging you aren't sure (giving yourself room to mess up) but also

TAKE INITIATIVE

taking steps forward. If we aren't uncomfortable, we aren't growing. We have to force ourselves into this sometimes by taking a leap into uncharted territory.

In business, there's *always* room for improvement. In my first book, *Interactive Project Management: Pixels, People, and Process,* my colleague Meghan McInerny and I talked about a process we developed and used at Clockwork. That process wasn't developed by just one person, or even just me and Meghan. It was a framework we established with help from many people over our early years of website and app development. When we started, there was *no* clear process (at our companies or elsewhere), and it was clear that we needed one. So we put something down on paper and evolved it over the years.

I wasn't the queen of process. In fact, most people will tell you that I often sidestep processes. But I saw that the people with whom we worked (software engineers, designers, etc.) and the people for whom we were doing the work (our clients) would benefit from a process. So I went for it. We went for it.

To act like a Boss, you have to find ways to initiate change or movement. Sometimes this is scary, and at other times it means doing something no one else wants to do (i.e., shit work). But I promise you that doing is always better than not doing. Stepping up to the plate and raising your hand to take on a challenge will put you in a better mindset and position on the other side.

You are the business, the business is you.

Taking initiative looks like:

- Doing what needs to be done.

- Improving what needs improvement.

- Noticing gaps that create inefficiencies or bad experiences for clients or customers.

- Worrying less about status or job titles and descriptions and more about the quality of the collective work and being part of something that makes a positive impact on the business around you.

- Acknowledging that there is no instruction manual. Test and try solutions without waiting for the perfect version.

- Sidestepping perceived barriers to good thinking and sharing ideas with others. New ideas will always challenge old ideas, so don't worry about pissing anyone off (you probably will).

You have the ability to change things, even if it's just within yourself. The idea that we don't have the ability to change things, that we are merely victims of established systems, is just not true. Every individual has power. If you're looking for permission, consider it granted ... by me!

Behave, but Don't "Behave"

We adopt this "I'm going to behave at work" attitude. And it sucks. It sucks for individuals and sucks for business.

"Behaving" goes back to our school days, especially for girls, who then grow into adults who behave. However, saying yes and putting our heads down, waiting for assignments, trying to appease an authority figure, and following the written rules to a T doesn't help us at work. Behaving teaches us how to avoid conflict, not walk into it. At work, challenging ideas and procedures produces better outcomes. Giving people what they want isn't necessarily giving people what they need. Behaving teaches us how to smile and not elevate concerns. Saying, "Matt's behavior in that meeting felt off; let's check in with the client to make sure things are running smoothly," feels like we're stabbing Matt in the back.

But here's the flip side: you have to play by human rules (like the Golden Rule) even when you're not playing by "the Rules." I am a misfit, and I often do things my way, but I am not rude or sneaky. I try to rock the boat by being unexpectedly good and by sharing out-of-the-box ideas that help.

How I misbehave goes back to my own value system and the self-culture I've cultivated over the years. I am committed to treating all people with respect and dignity, even when I am very frustrated. I am dedicated to outcomes more than a particular path for getting there. So my behavior might stray from the way things have "always" been done, but it doesn't stray from what I believe as a person and how I want to develop my work relationships and my work reputation.

Owning your shit doesn't mean mouthing off or going rogue. It means investing in relationships, building trust, and collaborating on other ways to be at work.

Persistence and Practice

After reading about these Boss qualities, some people might say, "I'm not wired like that!" First, I'd say, "Duh, Debbie, no one is!" Then I'd say, "You can be!"

How you approach the world and work takes practice. Our families of origin and our first bosses shaped us in ways that are ingrained in us as indelible imprints on the attitudes we bring to work. And they are rarely positive. That baggage comes with us from job to job—just think of all the invisible baggage in a five-person meeting. Every microaggression, every time we got overlooked, every time someone took credit for our idea, every time we were blamed for something someone else did, every time we tried and didn't succeed, every boss that was on a power trip. Times five! Practicing is important because it's never just *us* we're dealing with. We can only start with ourselves, but there is a lot going on that we can't control.

One of my superpowers is delivering hard messages. (I'll let you in on some of my secrets in chapter 6.) After a meeting in which I told a client some hard news, a colleague said that I give feedback like I breathe: naturally and without visible effort. She added, "It's not like that for other people." I believe her on both counts, but only because I have practiced this skill very consciously for twenty years. I learned through experience how to come into those conversations with energy that will *work*. And I learned that by having a lot of conversations in which my energy didn't work.

So we have to rewire ourselves. That's all! I have left jobs because my boss was a jackass, but not everyone sees that jackassery; some think "that's just work." It's not, but our attitudes can make a difference.

Ask for What You Want

Here's where I get a little therapist-y. You are an empowered person. You matter and you are valuable. (Google Stuart Smalley. He will remind you.) Own that fact.

Work just "happens" to most people—they drift through their careers, victims of their own assumptions of powerlessness. And I can't blame them for those assumptions. We live in a society that tells most people that they aren't the decision-makers and never will be.

But here's the secret: your decisions have just as much impact as those of anyone around you. If you started showing up to work dressed in a full suit every day, people would notice and talk, right? Because you are an influential part of the team. Take the initiative to suggest the changes that you want.

The closest someone can get to an ideal job is a role where they:

- take risks,

- are challenged and challenge themselves,

- learn,

- and can get better.

The closest someone can get to an ideal workplace is an environment where they feel:

- encouraged,

- valued,

- respected,

- and rewarded for curiosity.

Figure out tangible ways to move the needle on whatever matters to you. Approach your boss, talk with your colleagues, and start modeling the behavior you want to experience from others.

You know, be the change you want to see in the world. Who said that . . . oh yeah, *Gandhi*. He was smart—listen to him!

Talk about It

If you've said more than two words about working like a Boss to someone else in your organization, you're already crushing it compared to most people. We need to create more space, more often, for conversations about how work is broken *and* how to fix it. We spend a lot of time on the work itself and forget that connecting with people and making incremental changes are part of the job.

And, of course, be willing to look at your own behavior as well as the company's actions. Remember: fix your shit before adjusting others'.

Be Where You Are

Remember Lizzo and all the joy her fans felt as she said, "The world is full of problems, but we can fix them if we start with ourselves." Find joy in change and all the fixing we need to do. Self-improvement can be an interesting journey if we let go of the pressure to be perfect, keep in mind that we're all works in progress, and find power in doing the work. Find joy in trying new things that might shift your outlook and mindset. If they fail, that's just data you can use.

I know that, to some degree, it doesn't matter how much beer or free snacks I offer my employees—there are still days when work will suck for them. But a healthy, positive culture makes even the worst days a hell of a lot easier. You're a part of that culture, so if it's going to be healthy and positive for you, you've gotta make sure you give a shit.

Maybe you hate your job, or your boss, or your office. If you can change it, then do that! But if you can't, identify your reason for showing up—beyond rent. Is it the product you're proud of, the team that makes you laugh, or the community you serve? Where are there sparks of joy in your day? I'm not talking never-ending orgasmic joy. Just some moments when you can say, "Damn, I'm energized by that."

Get up in the morning and create a situation that succeeds within whatever barriers exist.

Work Like a Boss Takeaways

1. You can control your self-culture and influence a microculture around you.
2. Find joy in making improvements in your work self and work life. Forty hours a week (and sometimes more) is a lot of time to spend at a place or in a state of mind that is terrible.
3. There is no magic fix, just a lot of trial and error. Be honest with yourself along the way, take action, and reflect on what you learned (or didn't).

Chapter Four

KICK YOUR FEAR
IN THE FACE

There's fear in business . . . ~~and we don't talk about it.~~ and we're going to talk all about it. This is the four-letter *f* word that is actually off-limits at work.

First, I want to clarify: I'm not talking about fear-based work cultures or bosses who use fear as a tool to "motivate" teams.[7] That's another topic worthy of discussion, but I'm going to focus on internal fear—the fear we create and feel within ourselves. Both types of fear are damaging and unproductive, but we can adjust internal fear.

Can you think of someone who (you think) fears less than you? Maybe it's someone you look up to who seems to move through life with confidence, like they have the world by the tail. I know several people like that. I probably don't know the person you're thinking of, but

---

7 For more on those environments, read Liz Ryan, "Ten Unmistakable Signs Of A Fear-Based Workplace," Forbes, March 7, 2017, https://www.forbes.com/sites/lizryan/2017/03/07/ten-unmistakable-signs-of-a-fear-based-workplace.

I still feel 100 percent confident in saying that they are insecure about many, many things. And that tail you think they're holding? It's just their reusable lunch bag. Or the blanket they scream into when they're frustrated. They are human too.

Fear and insecurity spare no one. I hear the "You're so confident!" comments, but I'm plagued with doubt. It's the inescapable reality of being human: wondering at least once a day if I'm doing something wrong. I think about my weight and my double chins, I worry about what people think when they look at me or hear my ideas, I am afraid my clothes aren't nice enough or fit the right "look." I have to talk myself into just about everything: I second-guess my appearances (Should I try harder?), my humor (Why did I say that?!), and my ideas (Was that stupid?). Yet I do talk myself into things. I leave the house, go to meetings, and say things out loud, and I haven't died yet.

Self-doubt and confidence can coexist if we don't let self-sabotage get in the way. Insecurity and being a Boss can coexist if we don't let fear get in the way.

I speak in front of groups all the time. Yet one recent talk stands out to me because I was terrified more than usual. The Public Radio Program Directors Association hired me as the keynote speaker for their daylong conference. The audience consisted entirely of public radio people. For me, that translates to super smart, super polished, and pretty serious. I was intimidated. I'm smart *enough*, but not very polished and generally unpredictable on the serious front. All of which I am okay with, but dang if this audience didn't just make me nervous. Of course, the night before I went and read an article titled "How to Know if You've Lost Your Audience." (Yeah, in hindsight it's really easy to see how this wasn't a smart idea.) The next morning, as I'm standing in front of these radio directors, that article is *all* I can think about. I think, "I've lost them. I've been up here twenty seconds and I managed to do all the things that the article said not to do." I finished the talk and—lo and behold—it was fine. It's like my insecurity, fear, and self-sabotage ganged up on me.

(I did receive one of my favorite feedback comments of all time from an audience member at that talk. They said I was "Fairly banal." I am a lot of things—negative and positive—but not banal. I really want to talk to that person—they must be awesome.)

I've gotten better at managing the insecurities and self-doubt that lead to fear, as many people do as they grow in age, position, and experience. But I sure wish more people would have honest conversations about their own fear. We all have it. All of us. And the fact is, *it is surmountable*.

Some people make it look like they've read the book on life or work. That's a smokescreen. There is no book. None of us knows what we're doing.

Examining Our Fear

There are so many things we don't talk about in business, but fear might be the biggest. It's *hard* to talk about fear. It's an emotion, so right off the bat, we're unlikely to bring it up in a professional situation. And yet, *thousands of business decisions are driven by fear every day*. A company backs out of a potentially great deal because of fear. A boss lays unfair blame on a direct report out of fear. An employee doesn't speak up in a meeting because of fear.

We have to talk about the *f* word. Let's talk the crap out of it.

Fear at Work: A Recipe
Mix:

- 1 part insecurity
- 1 part "Don't bring personal things to work"
- Dash of change aversion

Garnish with perfectionism and enjoy! Served best with a side of self-sabotage to ensure you never change and your animal brain wins.

Fear at Work

1 part Insecurity
1 part "Don't bring personal things to work"
Dash of change aversion
Garnish with perfectionism
Enjoy!

The CliffsNotes Version of Fear

Fear is complicated. A lot of things make us afraid. There are some very common and obvious things, such as spiders, heights, and speaking in front of groups. But humans also have fear and anxiety around more ambiguous things. For example, we hear phrases like *afraid of failure* or *afraid of success*. Whether these threats are real or perceived gives little solace to our brains; we fear them, so our bodies go into fear mode.[8]

Science says that studying fear is not easy because the boundary between fear and anxiety is tenuous.[9] What's more, fear is interrelated with a lot of other feelings and states of mind, such as insecurity, shame,

8 Many articles explain how fear works in our brain and the biological, chemical, psychological, and emotional impact it has on us. I am not going to go into all that here because I'm not an expert and others explain it far better. Just search for it, and you will be rewarded with a range of interesting things to read.

9 Mary C. Lamia, "The Complexity of Fear," Psychology Today, December 15, 2011, https://www.psychologytoday.com/us/blog/intense-emotions-and-strong-feelings/201112/the-complexity-fear.

nervousness, perfectionism, and more. So I am using it here as a stand-in for that cocktail of complexity that follows us around. It can be overt or covert in how we feel it and how it shows up. It's sneaky and hard to pin down.

I found that when I start to talk about this with my colleagues and friends, everyone can see it. It *is* hard to articulate, and yet it makes sense. We can recall a person, maybe even ourselves, who has acted on fear at work. So read on and see yourself or a peer or a friend in what I'm saying. Have empathy, and then figure out how to kick that fear in the face.

Fear at Work

There are endless and diverse things to be afraid of. But at work, aside from the too-common "speaking in front of groups," I see fears clumped into a few broad categories that are the result of that mix of other feelings (insecurity, shame, etc.). They are not entirely independent of each other. Like most ambiguous things, our fears are interrelated and their origins are not always clear. Luckily, we don't need to diagnose fear to that degree to survive it—but more on that later. Let's start with the types of fear I see the most.

We Fear Conflict

This is a huge one. I've come to realize that most people feel that anything other than "That's great!" is conflict. "What information are you basing that on?" Conflict. "I disagree, I've been thinking about it a different way." Conflict. "It makes me feel bad when you take credit for my ideas." Conflict.

Conflict and confrontation present huge obstacles for many people. Yet at work, most of the situations we perceive as conflict or confrontation aren't terribly aggressive. We very seldom see a physical altercation or a passionate screaming match. Rather, we see opinions that push another person to explain themselves more clearly, comments that require a colleague to reflect on their actions or motivations, or questions that force a teammate to consider an alternate perspective.

In other words, most conflicts or confrontations are really just conversations. Human conversations. Think of your greatest and most successful nonwork relationships, like those with a partner, best friend, or close family member. Do those relationships ever involve pushing someone to see something a different way? Do you ever have to respectfully call out an idea or behavior that will help them understand it differently? Of course. You and this person likely share some degree of trust and intimacy, which grew from engaging in dialogue similar to what we would call *conflict* or *confrontation* at work.

The fear of conflict relates to how bad most people are at productively engaging with divergent ideas and perspectives. We assume that questioning someone's assumptions or disagreeing with a colleague is a bad thing. But that's just stuff we're projecting onto what could be a useful exchange of information resulting in a better outcome . . . *if* we get over our fear and have the conversation.

We assume conflict is bad, unhealthy, damaging, or—and this is where it cuts a little deeper—insulting and personal. Whether we are the person initiating the "conflict" or the person receiving it, these conversations bring up all kinds of feelings that trigger a range of behaviors. I have seen defensiveness, deflection, victimhood, denial, and more. But I have also seen interest, acceptance, curiosity, and connection. Some of it comes down to how you approach a conversation (more on that in chapter 6), but a lot of it comes down to how the other person accepts it, and that's out of your control. But don't fear that: fear never saying what needs to be said.

Conflict fear sounds like:

"I'm sure I will just get used to it."

"She probably thought it all through, I won't ask."

"It's fine. Really, it's fine."

"I don't agree, but it's their idea."

We're afraid of pissing people off or hurting their feelings, and we have to get over that. Nothing good ever came from sitting on your hands as a bad idea unfolds in front of you.

We're Afraid We're Not Good Enough

This one is a doozy. Many "enoughs" plague us, but most boil down to one in particular: good enough. There's the performance side of good: smart enough, talented enough, knowledgeable enough, accomplished enough, and on and on. There is also the value side of good: not worthy enough or undeserving. The roots of these fears run deep (damn you, families of origin!), but we let them get in our way more than we know at work.

We have imposter syndrome, we are filled with self-doubt, and we rely on others to do something we *could* do. This fear keeps us from speaking up when we have an idea or need to make a point. It keeps us from offering to do something valuable because we're afraid we won't do it well. It keeps us from demonstrating our skills at work because we don't have the confidence to believe in them. Lastly, this fear cultivates submissiveness and deference within us.

I had a colleague—let's call her Ann—who worked on a project for three years. She had gotten to know the client's team very well. As is usual with any team, it was full of different personality and communication types, and it had a variety of stakeholders. Ann got along with most of the team swimmingly, but there was one client with whom she had a difficult time. I was brought in more than once to talk to that person and reset the energy because my colleague was constantly feeling defeated.

The troublemaker wasn't really that bad. Yes, she was negative and didn't effuse cheerful energy (or words), but she was relatively harmless. Yet Ann had built up fear around talking to this client. The fear was rooted in Ann's feeling that she was not good enough to do it. Ann would tell me, "You're just so good at those kinds of conversations." Yet her admiration for the skill didn't translate to action; she wouldn't try because she was too afraid. She let the fear control how she behaved, and, as often happens with fear, it perpetuated (and worsened) what she desperately wanted to change.

I have seen this happen over and over. The "I'm not good enough" or "I don't really deserve to be here" nugget in the animal brain takes over and wins. With fear of the "enoughs" especially, the impact seems to compound. It becomes so big that overcoming it feels impossible. And the patterns that emerge along the way are increasingly difficult to revert. Ann hadn't stood up for herself and her ideas for three years. How do you change course?! How do you stand up and say something after so long?!

You just try. As I was writing this chapter, my spouse forwarded me an email newsletter that she receives. Its heading read, "Often, in walking through our fear, we discover that the strength of our fright was out of sync with reality."[10] While we spend a lot of time worrying about all the possibilities, we miss the opportunity to act and to prove our fears wrong.

This fear sounds like:

"My idea probably isn't that good."

"That other person should take the lead. She knows more."

"I just don't think I'm right for that position."

We Fear What Others Will Think about Us

We are all very concerned about what people think of us. On the one hand, it's very human to worry about that because we're social beings; we need people to like us to survive. But every day, in every office, people shut down their own words and actions because they are afraid of what other people will think of them. We think we will look [*insert negative characteristic here*]. Maybe you've thought you might look inexperienced, too young or too old, too dumb or even too smart (this shows up most often in women navigating patriarchal power structures), or too much.

I bet you have shut down some part of you at work, even in the past week, because of the fear of looking bad. The result is twofold: not only

---

10 From the DailyOM newsletter, by Madisyn Taylor, sent on October 31st, 2019.

did you silence something that could have added value, but everyone around you also lost the opportunity to see it.

We can't be *too* anything, right? What would people think?! Well, I've been *too* my whole life. Too loud, too butch, too fat, too direct, too, too, too. I once worked with a woman—I will call her Katherine—who shamed me when she thought I was being *too*. In a group meeting, she'd say, "Oh, Nancy," and gently shake her head after I said something direct or critical (which happened regularly). I can still hear it now: "Oh, Nancy." Each time, it felt loaded and I felt shame. What it felt like she was actually saying was, "You aren't acting like a conventional woman in a conventional Midwestern, passive-aggressive meeting, and I'm uncomfortable and it's not how I would act so I feel like I must shame you and try to put you in the narrow place from which I operate." I mean, I now see that "Oh, Nancy" was a far more efficient phrase, but I still loathe it.

Policing happens to women all the time. I see it, and I've felt it. When we were children we were told to be "ladylike" or say something only if we had something "nice" to say. Our mothers sprinkled us with "What will people think?!" after criticizing something we were doing that was inevitably not really all that bad, like pulling up our uncomfortable tights. We've internalized such commentary so thoroughly that we now police ourselves through this type of fear. Go back to the personal

values we discussed earlier in the book and let them be the way you police yourself. They represent the person you actually want to be, not the person guided by fears of what someone will think of you.

Wanting to be liked will compromise your success. Wanting to appeal to everyone will not make you friends or allies at work. Being respectfully yourself will serve you better.

This fear sounds like:

"I might sound dumb."

"I don't want to take up too much time."

"What if it's a bad idea?!"

We Fear We'll Do the Wrong Thing

In school, quizzes always had a correct answer and assignments had instructions. As kids, we were punished for not following the very specific rules that were laid out for us. This continued at some of the early jobs we had as teens. Then, somewhere in adulthood, we got jobs where we had to start taking initiative and deciding rather than being told what to do. And boy, was that a hard change. Some didn't fare very well. This leads to the fourth common fear I see: fear of doing the wrong thing.

As a CEO, this is the fear I see the most in my colleagues. And as an entrepreneur, it's the fear that is most foreign to me. I started a company because I *couldn't* be told what to do. Now I work with people who wish that someone would tell them what to do. But I've come to realize that entrepreneurs don't think of right and wrong—within the context of work and decision-making—as black-and-white terms as much as many other people do. Perhaps it's because we've failed so many times that we've had to learn to value it.

When we don't have a road map or a set of instructions, some people cave under the pressure of doing the *right* thing. Yet, most jobs in the twenty-first century have a degree of ambiguity to them. It varies between industry, between the "collar" types (white-collar, blue-collar, no-collar, or new-collar), and between roles within an organization. But nearly every job requires us to make some best guesses to get things done.

We assume that, aside from one single thing that smart people would know to do, everything else is wrong. Here's what I've noticed: if there is not an obvious *right* way, then there are many right ways. If A and B both seem viable and possible, then maybe either is "right."

Perfection isn't real. Failure and iteration are. I'm not saying to run out and start failing every which way. I'm saying that you will learn more from trying and failing than from not doing anything because you're afraid. Aside from terribly punitive workplaces, if you use logic and rationale to make a sound decision, a failure will be tolerated. It might even be celebrated if you share what you learned in the process! (This rule may not apply to some professions. Like brain surgery. If you're a brain surgeon, in some cases, failure may be a problem. Just sayin'.)

This fear sounds like:

"I just don't know what to do."

"I wish there were a clear step."

"I don't have enough information to do anything."

Like I said earlier in the book, oftentimes doing something—anything—is the right thing because there is no other way to make progress. The fantasy work manual would just say, "Start trying." Yoda would say, "Do. Or do not. There is no try." Either way, movement is essential.

We Fear the Unknown or Unfamiliar

Humans are wired for homeostasis. Our minds and bodies will try to maintain the status quo at all costs. That means unfamiliar or uncharted territory can put many of us into fear mode. We almost never know what will *really* happen after we make any decision, but at work, this reality seems to trip us up.

This fear is deeply intertwined with the other common fears. It causes all the what-ifs we ask ourselves. We aren't sure what lies on the other side of a decision or an action, and that's difficult for us. So we don't do anything; we become complacent. This fear keeps us making predictable choices. This fear puts comfort first, at all costs. We've all heard the saying, "The devil you know is better than the devil you don't." We seem to blanket-apply that at work.

Fear keeps us from our better selves. And sometimes, the idea of succeeding is the thing we fear the most. If we succeed, more will be expected of us. If we succeed, we are more likely to face further challenges. If we succeed, it changes people's impression of us. If we succeed, we'll be pushed into more discomfort. If we succeed, what is expected of us will change.

Fear is complex and woven into the experiences and lessons we've carried with us for years. We can't just shed it without effort. I know that. I have spent time and energy working on my own fears, so I can say with confidence that it takes intention and attention. And yet we can all remember a time in our lives when we beat fear. We all have personal case studies of success, of overcoming something, and of making it through something we dreaded.

The anticipation of the thing you fear is worse than the thing itself.

The Manifestations of Fear

Objectively, fear isn't a bad thing. Like our negativity bias, it comes from and operates within the more instinctual parts of our brains. It helps us respond to danger. Thanks, fear! But our basic little brains send up too many danger signals, often when there is no actual threat—like when we're about to present to a large audience. Sad trombone.

As an owner of a company, I've watched hundreds of thousands of dollars be spent on people not dealing with their fear. Any of the fears I shared earlier can lead to the fearful responses of fight, flight, or freeze. We may not feel overtly afraid of a client or the magnitude of a project, yet we might exhibit behaviors that look like fear responses: avoidance or indecisiveness. We may not feel afraid of success, but we find ourselves stuck about a decision that would put us in the spotlight.

Fear—and the actions we do or don't take because of it—shapes us in ways of which we may not be aware. Here's what I see.

Fight at Work: Territorialism and Defensiveness

This is an easy one. We've seen it in meetings and side conversations. I'm afraid that what I just said sounded dumb, so I follow up with, "Well, I formed my opinion based on the data John passed around last week," implying that John's data might be bad. Or we're afraid our colleague came off as smarter during the presentation, so we hoard information from her the next week, only to mention it in a meeting to sound in the know.

Be honest: you've done something like those examples. We all have.

The fight response can be directed at a person or thing or it can be vague. But hoarding, drawing harsh boundaries within a project or team, getting territorial about who owns what information, and refusal to collaborate are all fight responses.

Flight at Work: Overanalyzing and Avoidance

This is a quieter response. People don't actually leave the workplace or quit. Instead, fleeing often disguises itself as hard work, but it's not productive work.

If someone is afraid of looking dumb or sounding unprepared, they will withdraw to their desks and perseverate on details. If they're afraid of the unfamiliar, they hash out every possible scenario and try to plan for any outcome. If they're afraid of doing the wrong thing, they will keep researching—in solitude—until they have "enough" information. (Spoiler: they will never feel like they have enough.)

Flighters might self-sabotage by simply avoiding the person or situation they fear. They will try to switch teams or not raise their hand to participate.

Freezing at Work: Indecision and Paralysis

Freezing, like fleeing, at work isn't literal. The freezers just don't do anything differently. They can't decide how or what to deal with, so they don't. It's like that urge to maintain the status quo at all costs.

Note that each of these fear responses involves paralysis. "The most concrete thing that neuroscience tells us is that when the fear system of the brain is active, exploratory activity and risk-taking are turned off."[11] So when we're in a state of fear, other cognitive activities that could benefit us at work, like brainstorming or making a decision and running with it, are basically paralyzed.

In *The Dance of Fear*, Harriet Lerner states, "It is not fear that stops you from doing the brave and true thing in your daily life. Rather, the problem is avoidance. You want to feel comfortable, so you avoid doing or saying the thing that will evoke fear and other difficult emotions.

11 Gregory Berns, "In Hard Times, Fear Can Impair Decision-Making," *New York Times*, December 6, 2008, https://www.nytimes.com/2008/12/07/jobs/07pre.html.

Avoidance will make you feel less vulnerable in the short run, but it will never make you less afraid."

The more we sit around fighting, fleeing, or freezing, the more we're digging ourselves into holes and habits that don't serve us. No one wants to be gripped by their fear. I see that in conversations I have with colleagues. People *want* to behave differently but are gripped by unarticulated fear.

> *Between our weaknesses and our insecurities, we convince ourselves that we can't or shouldn't. That we'll fail or are undeserving. That's not true.*

Fearing Less

All we can hope for and do is fear fear less (that's not a typo—read it again). Bosses aren't fearless; no one is. Despite how it looks to outsiders, they experience the same ebb and flow of all the emotions we've talked about in this chapter: the self-doubt, insecurity, shame, and vulnerability. The difference is that they've figured out how not to let it get in their way for too long.

When I was writing this chapter, I had the gut feeling that my advice couldn't just be "Get over it!" What assuaged that reaction is that we *need* fear. Being fearless isn't the goal; our goal is to understand and deal with the fear.

Fear is a driving force in how we act, make decisions, and relate to people—at work and elsewhere. It's also biological and deeply rooted in parts of our brain that are as old as humankind. There are numerous websites (thousands, in fact) that explain how fear works better than I ever could in a short book about work. If you have fears, I encourage you to read a few. Boiling it down to the biology really puts things into perspective and gives you something to point to the next time you're feeling fearful. ("Oh, there's my amygdala acting up again, that sneaky bugger!") For now, I'll explain very briefly.

Fear resides within the amygdala, a part of our instinctual and emotional brain, which "talks" to the rational part of our brain (the frontal cortex) when we experience fear-inducing stimuli. This dialogue occurs over seconds—milliseconds, even! But this back-and-forth is important because our biology is essentially sorting out what to do. The brain is determining whether the stimuli are an actual threat or just appear that way.

When the amygdala is damaged, we can't make decisions very well. It's like our "gut" or instincts are all tied up in the same area of the brain as our fear. And we need this feedback loop to make timely, appropriate, and smart decisions. In other words, the rational part of our brain isn't the center of decision-making; it is the dialogue between reason and emotion that helps us make good decisions.[12] So fear isn't bad! Yay! But you have to know how to work with it. Cheesy sayings like "If it makes you uncomfortable, you're growing" have a kernel of truth.

Some of us fear many things, some fewer. Regardless of a fear's origins, our predilection for fear influences our decisions and our outlook. Mary Lamia explains, "When an emotion is triggered, it has an impact on our judgments and choices in situations. In a study of risk-taking, participants who were fearful consistently made judgments and choices that were relatively pessimistic and amplified their perception of risk in a given situation, in contrast to happy or angry participants who were more likely to disregard risk by making relatively optimistic judgments and choices. . . . Thus, awareness of your emotions and considering how they might influence your decision-making in a given situation is important in your approach to life, your work, and your goals."[13] This demonstrates what I see over and over again at work: fear perpetuates negativity, which perpetuates fear, and on and on. Kate Murphy notes that "arresting an overactive amygdala requires first realizing and then

---

12 Gardiner Morse, "Decisions and Desire," *Harvard Business Review* (January 2006), https://hbr.org/2006/01/decisions-and-desire.

13 Mary C. Lamia, "The Complexity of Fear," *Psychology Today,* December 15, 2011, https://www.psychologytoday.com/us/blog/intense-emotions-and-strong-feelings/201112/the-complexity-fear.

admitting you're feeling uneasy and scared."[14] And thus begins the work on fearing less.

Because this isn't a manual for everything, I am going to focus on two of my favorite and most effective ways to overcome fear. I've thought about them a lot, used them myself, and watched colleagues and friends embrace them over the years. The strongest cures for fear are better self-talk and building resilience.

Talking Ourselves into Confidence, or at Least Less Insecurity

Fear at work grows the fastest and gnarliest in the stories we tell ourselves. We've inherited these stories from our families, teachers, popular culture, friends, strangers, and social groups. We learned explicit lessons and implicit mores about how to think, behave, talk, walk, and interact. Much of this wasn't about work at all, but we tow a large bag of it along with us wherever we go. As we discussed in the "Own Your Shit" chapter, we, as adults, have to do the hard work of unraveling, examining, and reconstructing what we've inherited. You must do this in order to bring what *you* want to work.

It starts with self-talk. Self-talk can be positive or negative. It can be

---

14 Kate Murphy, "Outsmarting Our Primitive Responses to Fear," *New York Times,* October 26, 2017, https://www.nytimes.com/2017/10/26/well/live/fear-anxiety-therapy. html.

productive and helpful, or it can undercut your confidence. It can boost you up or sabotage everything you do. We can focus on our strengths instead of wallowing in weakness. And the biggest takeaway is that you have total control over your self-talk.

Psychologists know the value and risk of self-talk. There are thousands of blog posts about self-talk on PsychologyToday.com. There are some common elements: self-talk can be damaging or beneficial, everyone engages in self-talk (good and bad), and the contents of self-talk are changeable.

Own Yourself

Before any self-talk changes, you have to believe that you have agency. This came up in the previous chapter, and it will come up again because it plagues people. I see a lack of agency in people of all ages and job ranks. I talk to people who seem to believe they don't have agency in their lives and their paths. And yet, they do. *You* do.

Therapist and author Pia Mellody said, "We are all valuable because we were born." You don't have to earn the right to act with agency, but you *do* have to act with agency for people to see that in you. I'm not saying that's fair—it would be satisfying if people defaulted to treating others as equals and with no pretense of power or territorialism, but for now, we don't live in that world.

As I've gotten older, I've learned to suppress the self-sabotage and negativity that results from insecurity. I try to contribute only when I think I have something of value to offer, but I spent years measuring my value on way too narrow a range. I'm getting better about recognizing value more broadly within work. If we never speak up, we won't know what we have to contribute.

What's the relationship between agency and fear? Believing in and acting from a place of agency reduces fear. If you believe you are an active agent in your life—that life doesn't just happen to you—there is less to fear. No one can take that from you once *you* believe it. Many of the stories we tell ourselves that generate fear revolve around losing control. If you start from a place of knowing that you drive your life, those fears will loosen their grip on you. As an article in *Smithsonian* explains, "When we are able to recognize what is and isn't a real threat, relabel an experience and enjoy the thrill of that moment, we are ultimately at a place where we feel in control. That perception of control is vital to how we experience and respond to fear. When we overcome the initial 'fight or flight' rush, we are often left feeling satisfied, reassured of our safety and more confident in our ability to confront the things that initially scared us."[15]

15 Arash Javanbakht and Linda Saab, "What Happens in the Brain When We Feel Fear," *Smithsonian Magazine*, October 27, 2017, https://www.smithsonianmag.com/science-nature/what-happens-brain-feel-fear-180966992/.

You can ask for what you want, but not by sitting around, complaining. You can have that tough conversation, but not by blaming the other person for everything. You can speak up in the meeting, but not by just talking to talk. You accomplish these things by practicing walking through the fears that lead us to act from places of territorialism, avoidance, or paralysis.

Build Resiliency to Bounce Back

Resiliency can both prevent and heal fear. It's a salve. The Resiliency Center defines resilience as "a human ability to recover quickly from disruptive change, or misfortune without being overwhelmed or acting in dysfunctional or harmful ways."[16] Fear freezes us, but resiliency counters that urge by giving us the sense that we will get through whatever we're afraid of and might even thrive afterward. It's the power of productive self-talk and self-care in action.[17] It allows us to recover quickly from both internal and external bumps in the road.

---

16 Al Siebert Resiliency Center, "Resiliency Definitions," https://resiliencycenter.com/resiliency-definitions/

17 Laura Starecheski, "Why Saying Is Believing—The Science Of Self-Talk," *Morning Edition*, NPR, October 7, 2014, https://www.npr.org/sections/health-shots/2014/10/07/353292408/why-saying-is-believing-the-science-of-self-talk.

As important as resiliency is for our minds, bodies, and success in the world, it's not something we're explicitly taught. (Are you starting to see a pattern about the things we are taught and the things we aren't?) As far back as I remember, no one talked about resiliency with me. Not as a kid in school as I struggled with paying attention and felt shame. Not in my twenties as I was coming out more publicly. Not in my thirties when

I was starting and running companies. Throughout all these experiences, I felt fear and stress and I never thought consciously about resiliency. It turns out that much of what it takes to be resilient—like curiosity, a sense of humor, and an action-oriented approach—are qualities I exhibited and learned along the way; they just weren't packaged as resiliency. I bet you possess these qualities too!

Having resiliency means trusting that everything will be okay in the end—and moving forward because of that trust. It's a helpful, internal voice that says, "You'll be fine. You'll figure this out," even when you don't know exactly how to do it at that moment. We have all heard stories of people making the best of terrible situations or using a stumble—even an all-out failure—as motivation to do even better. Lot of people have looked adversity in the face and come out on top. (Have you heard of Oprah Winfrey? Yeah, me too.)

People throughout history have experienced major traumas and come out on the other side—much to our respect and awe—with composure, compassion, and strength. The resilience a woman draws on to recover from debilitating injury after a terrible accident requires strategies we can also use at work every day: positivity, learning from experiences, being open to people and situations, and more.[18]

We might think we're not wired like that, but no one is. It's a muscle that some individuals have strengthened over time through practice. According to the American Psychological Association, resilience isn't something we have or don't have. Resilience "involves behaviors, thoughts, and actions that can be learned and developed in anyone."[19]

Why do we need resilience at work? Because work is physically and mentally stressful, often exacerbated by the types of fear we feel. We can help our bodies and minds by growing and flexing our resiliency muscle. Most adults like routine and familiarity, but in order to accomplish what *really* needs to happen at work—do better, work faster, produce more, innovate, compete—we have to adapt to new things. It is unlikely that we will do one thing, every day, for thirty years. In our new work era,

18 Jessie Sholl, "The 5 Best Ways to Build Resiliency," *Experience Life*, September 2011, https://experiencelife.com/article/the-5-best-ways-to-build-resiliency/.

19 American Psychological Association, "Building Your Resilience," February 1, 2020, https://www.apa.org/topics/resilience.

we have to be brave enough to bring up new ideas and resilient enough to recover if they don't succeed. We have to react to change within our organizations with an open mind, ready to start learning whatever is next on the horizon.

April Seifert is a woman who both lives and champions resiliency. She is an amazing person, an accomplished professional, and an inspiring life design strategist. She's done a TEDx talk, has a podcast that features strong women in our community, and cofounded Peak Mind, a center for psychological strength. She did all this after overcoming some very difficult life events: when she was eleven years old, her father died, and as a teenager, she was diagnosed with multiple sclerosis.

What I admire isn't just that she overcame these obstacles, but that she put them to use for herself. Her fascination and expertise are in "mental dark matter," a psychological analogy to the dark matter that scientists estimate accounts for up to 85 percent of our universe. This material is made of up of particles that can't be seen, but we know they are there. For April, this is a perfect analogy to our subconscious mind, which dutifully works away at creating shortcuts and constructing truths that help us be more efficient in our chaotic world.

"Our mental dark matter sends us thoughts and feelings that are not always helpful and likely aren't true," April explains. "They created maladaptive self-policing limitations that lead us to be self-critical and to believe that we deserve less than we really do. And the worst, to live a passive half-life wasting the beautiful opportunity we have in front of us."[20] Our fear is often wrapped up in these cannots and should-nots.

Resiliency is an opportunity to be our better selves. The fear that keeps us from putting ourselves out there, the people who *will* push our buttons, and the business expectations that continue to rise and change aren't going away. But learning to cope with this—building your resiliency—will allow you to tap into and own your power at work more easily.

What Does Resiliency Look Like?

Like so many things related to our brains, emotions, and mental health, resilience doesn't look the same for every person, nor is it achieved in the same way. Like the fear it can help you overcome, your path to practicing resilience and how you find success will be uniquely yours. Yep, again, it's on you to figure out.

---

20 April Seifert., "Mind Over [Dark] Matter: A Guide to Uncovering Your True Potential," TEDxMahtomedi, November 25, 2019, https://www.youtube.com/watch?v=hTnSX4sY-QhU&t; and April Seifert, "Build Psychological Strength to Become an Active Participant in Your Life," DisruptHR Talks, November 6, 2019, https://disrupthr.co/vimeo-video/build-psychological-strength-to-become-an-active-participant-in-your-life-april-seifert-disrupthr-talks/.

As a starting point, we can look at a 2003 study that outlined the primary characteristics of resilient people.[21]

- Viewing change as a challenge or opportunity
- Commitment
- Recognition of limits to control
- Engaging the support of others
- Close, secure attachment to others
- Personal or collective goals
- Self-efficacy
- Ability to get stronger in response to stress
- Ability to reflect on past successes
- Realistic sense of control and having choices
- Sense of humor
- Action-oriented approach

21 Conner, K. M., MD, and Jonathan, D. R., MD, "Development of a New Resilience Scale: The Connor-Davidson Resilience Scale (CD-RISC)," *Depression and Anxiety* 18, no. 2 (2003): 76–82.

- Patience

- Tolerant of negative setbacks

- Adaptability to change

- Optimism

- Faith

Obviously, no one exhibits all of the qualities in every moment, but together they begin to draw a map for bouncing back from obstacles. Interestingly, the same study found "it is possible to perform well in one area, such as work, in the face of adversity, but function poorly in another area, such as personal relationships."[22] My hunch is that at some point you've put resilience skills to work in areas of your life outside the office. I get it: it's much more natural to think about emotional development in your personal life than in your professional life. But, if we're going to start tearing down those personal and professional walls, we have to own every aspect of it, including personal development *at* work.

Resilience is as social as it is psychological. It's something we do for and by ourselves, but we inevitably look to our community to support

---

22 Leslie Riopel, "Resilience Skills, Factors and Strategies of the Resilient Person," *Positive Psychology,* April 7, 2019, https://positivepsychology.com/resilience-skills/.

us along the way. A few years ago, I saw Sheryl Sandberg speak at a smallish event in Minneapolis. She was promoting and speaking about her book *Option B: Facing Adversity, Building Resilience, and Finding Joy*, which was about her husband's death and how she managed it emotionally, professionally, and psychologically. The event took place about eighteen months after the death, and I was struck by her composure. She was petite, kind-looking, and glowing in an all-white outfit. She also had a commanding presence—you *wanted* to listen to her. I had forgotten that her husband was from the Twin Cities. When she told the crowd that she had been having a flood of memories since arriving, she was crying, sharing, and getting very personal among this group of strangers. The fact that she was a powerful woman at one of the world's most powerful companies faded into the background, and all I saw was a vulnerable person sharing hard stories with us.

One of the details I remember most from her talk and *Option B* is how much Sandberg opened up and reached out to her community in order to persevere personally. When we think of resilience, we often focus on the individual ways *we* need to get better or all the things *we* have to improve. But we can also make progress personally by focusing on our social and communal surroundings. The support, energy, presence, and goodwill of the people *around* us fuel resiliency *within* us. It stands to reason that if communities help build resiliency, building community at work will also build resiliency at work. Creating a community at work helps us get past the inevitable bumps, the times when we fail and make mistakes. Our community can help us live resiliently and move through those situations more healthily and more successfully. As we do this, we also build up the resilience of the community.

I was grateful to Sandberg for writing the book. I've thought a lot about resilience over the years as I moved through difficult times or tried to help others move through the natural fits and starts of professional life. She brought such a high profile to the subject with such humanity. It was the reminder we all need about the power and ability we each have to exercise our individual resiliency muscles. She acknowledged her own devastation and her inability to see past that devastation for a time. In her book, she recognized that we all have the ability to survive and to build ourselves back up after hard times. We all have opportunities to tap into our inner strength and the strength of those around us to remember what we're made of and move past the tough stuff.

Sandberg proved with the book, and in her talk, that resilience isn't an always-on thing. Like happiness, it's not a place you get to once and remain forever. It's something you work on, exercise, and remind your-self to cultivate all the time. Sometimes you just cry because it's hard. But, at the end of the day, we are equipped with raw instincts. We have the ability to fight, figure things out, and talk ourselves into whatever is next. We also have the ability to improve as we do all that. I think that's what Sandberg was writing about and reminding us readers about.

How to Build It

There are thousands of resources that you can use to build resiliency, so if this topic is speaking to you, you have a lot of material to work with. Here are a few that resonate with me, personally.

The American Psychological Association has a list of steps you can take to build resilience.[23] My favorites for work are "keep things in perspective" and "avoid negative outlets." This isn't a surprise, I'm sure, given how much I've talked about both of these subjects. It's really easy to catastrophize what happens at work, but if you talk to people around you about whatever happened, you'll probably find that someone has been through something similar. To maintain perspective, talk to that person and not the naysayers who will go down a rabbit hole of negativity with you.

Jenny Evans is a speaker, author, and expert on physiology and chemistry as it relates to resiliency, confidence, and performance. The author of *The Resiliency rEvolution: Your Stress Solution for Life 60 Seconds at a Time*, she takes a very psychological approach to resiliency and reducing

---

23 American Psychological Association, "Building Your Resilience," February 1, 2020, https://www.apa.org/topics/resilience.

stress (which is, after all, a chemical experience). To avoid the negative effects of stress, she recommends using as little as thirty to sixty seconds of intense physical activity to lower stress and build chemical resiliency.

Take a curious and learning-centered approach to events. Reflect on what you can learn from what happened, ask questions that inspire introspection instead of self-criticism, and look for opportunities for self-discovery. If you focus on growth, rather than perfection or acceptance, it's a lot easier to take unexpected and even unfortunate events and use them for good.

You can get further than you think by applying whatever work you're already doing in your personal life to your work self too. Fighting, surviving, and resilience-building don't just happen after hours. They happen at work too, and bringing the awareness, the compassion, and the skills Sandberg talks about to difficult times at work is very Boss.

Kick Fear in the Face by Staring It Down

To people wondering how they got to the metaphorical table: the reality is, it doesn't matter. You're there. You can let imposter syndrome take over, or you can take advantage of the opportunity, do your homework, work hard, and use the job to get the experience that you feel like you're lacking. Work isn't about what you know; it's about what you deliver.

To people worried about anything less than perfection: trapping yourself with expectations of immediate excellence only guarantees mediocrity. A consistent 99 percent of innovation is failure, and if your company isn't embracing that mentality, it's on you to be willing to fail within your own day-to-day activities. New attempts lead to new mistakes . . . but new mistakes lead to better outputs.

Don't talk yourself out of an opportunity because you don't believe you are worthy or capable of it or because you're worried about what people will think or how you will look. Trust yourself to show up. Confidence and credibility go hand in hand, and confidence building requires you to put yourself into uncomfortable situations and work hard to learn and grow—to become resilient.

Resiliency allows you to stand square in the face of fears, challenges, and uncomfortable ideas and say, "How can we make each other better?"

Work Like a Boss Takeaways

1. Fear influences nearly everything we do at work, consciously or unconsciously. We let it affect so much of what we do that it's almost second nature.
2. Bosses aren't fearless, but they fear less.
3. We each have the power to reframe all the fear that's controlling us.

Chapter Five
EMBRACE THE MESS

Work is messy. We try to ignore that it's full of uncertainty, emotion, and volatility. We try to ignore that business as we know it is mostly about relationships, experiments, and best guesses. We mask—or try to manage—this messiness with policies, strategy documents, layers of hierarchy, rules, verbose objectives, and software. We have unspoken rules around what professionalism looks like and sounds like to override individualism. We have processes and requirements, such as educational degrees, based on tradition rather than evidence. We unsuccessfully try to leave our personal lives behind when we walk into the office.

Work is messy because people are messy and, when it comes down to it, work is just a bunch of people trying to get stuff done. The business side of business is the easiest part of our working world. The human side is where things get hard.

We all know people are messy and weird. Believe it or not, *you* are messy and weird. It's not just them. It's not just you. It's all humans because humans are weird. We all have individual quirks that influence how we talk, act, and interpret the world around us, *and* we're unpredictable! When we put a bunch of people together and force them to share space, interact, and collaborate, the mess grows exponentially. I'm not saying this to be negative: it's simply true. You've probably seen and felt it too. Working with ten people on a project is harder than working with three, and the project will definitely take longer to complete.

So here we are—basically ignoring these messes—because we spend so much time and energy on the wrong things.

We Focus on Things Instead of People

We often think that things—gadgets, programs, or software—will bridge gaps and make people work together better in organizations and teams. Leaders try to solve problems with collaboration or feedback software, new office layouts, professional development events, written policies, and process consultants. Leadership teams and executives launch big initiatives or invest in new technologies that take hundreds of thousands of dollars and years to build, all in attempts to solve people problems. I see it all the time. When I mention this to clients or to an audience, there is an audible collective sigh. Sometimes I even say it in meetings with clients who want to buy that technology from me.

I once had a client who was dead set on hiring my team to build a collaboration tool from scratch to help their teams communicate better with each other (this was before Slack). I asked if their teams were communicating without the tool, and they said no. If communication isn't happening, it's not because people are missing a tool. People will find ways to share ideas if they want to share ideas. But no tool will enable behavior that isn't already occurring.

This shortcutting is happening everywhere. How many companies have invested in a customer relationship management (CRM) system instead of thinking about how to actually develop relationships—the oh-so-critical *R* in *CRM*? Many.

Leaders who do this aren't dumb—they are human. Individuals also turn to thing solutions when trying to crack the code on a work problem. If this Gantt chart were better, we would have hit the deadline. If there were a policy about PTO, my team wouldn't have been gone during those pivotal meetings. If our content management system were better, we wouldn't have approval delays. Yet hitting deadlines, meeting effectiveness, and content approvals are all human problems.

Things will never fix work. Thing-based solutions are only as good as the people using them and will only reflect the way people are *already* working. Most people have a near-constant desire to focus more and plan better. To get there, they often search for apps that track how we spend our time or planners with magical layouts that will take us from chaos to clarity. In reality, both focus and planning are about habits: only improving behaviors will fix either problem. Things might help facilitate that, but they won't (and can't) do the actual work.

When we focus on the things, we divert our attention from details that can have a more powerful impact: the inspiration and purpose behind whatever it is we're asking or doing, the big idea and vision that generate motivation in other people, and the why that connects individuals to actions. All the *human* stuff.

We Settle into the Status Quo

People gravitate toward groupthink but want to be individuals. People judge others for being different but hate being judged. People want things to change but are often the barrier to it. The "way things are" doesn't usually serve the greatest good, yet alternatives are few and far between. This is all true, especially at work.

While working on this chapter, I saw a tweet that encapsulated so much of what I had been thinking about. It read, "There's a guy in my office everyone shittalks for taking lots of sick days & bathroom breaks, like the accepted narrative is that he's a lazy fuckup. And then I put pieces together & realized the dude has ulcerative colitis. The cult of work suuuucks."[24] And there it is: the "cult of work." The homogenization of our actions, appearances, and behaviors at work is so thorough that we judge everyone around us for something as inconsequential as going to the bathroom more frequently than we do. Twentieth-century professionalism is still so ingrained in our offices that it forces us, either implicitly or explicitly, to behave in a very specific way—and is basically a cult.

You might be thinking, "That's so extreme, my office isn't like that!" but I am willing to bet that you follow some unspoken norms or expectations there that are more rigid than necessary if the *primary* interest is actually getting work done well. Maybe it's what's deemed appropriate attire (believe it or not, you can get as much work done in comfortable clothes as you can suits and skirts). Maybe it's what time your butt is expected to be in a particular seat or the way you speak (must sound college educated!) or wear your hair (must be "neat and clean"!). I've heard stories from women about feeling like they have to wear some makeup to work in order to look acceptable.

We figure (and are told) that we have to toe the line if we want to get ahead, and so we do. Most of us don't have the guts, or diplomacy, or interest, or wherewithal to break up the norms, so they endure. You might

24 Jake Paul Sartre (@PissJugTycoon), Twitter, December 27th, 2019, 10:29 p.m., https://twitter.com/PissJugTycoon/status/1210779745031352321.

not even be completely aware of it because it's "just the way things are." I've seen it, and I get it. These norms never worked for me.

As I grew my company, I was very outspoken about encouraging people to do what *they* needed to do in order to get their best work done. I meant everything from what they wore to where they worked to how they connected with clients. I wanted every person to be free from worry about fitting in or doing things the same as everyone else. Once people can stop worrying about that, they have more time to think about what really matters: doing good work. I don't care if you're in cargo shorts or if you take naps under your desk. I care whether you get your work done well and contribute great ideas.

The thing about the illusion of sameness and the rigidity of the status quo is that it's false. And it keeps so much of the good parts of people out of the office. We aren't robots, and that's a good thing. We are all unique and varied and think, talk, act, and engage in specific ways. The sooner we learn how to bring that out in ourselves and others, and embrace it, the sooner we'll get to a much healthier way of working. Can we do that? Please?

The way things have always been done will not get us to a new place. It will keep things exactly as they are. The human stuff is messy stuff. It's easier to talk about the financial goals, Q2 stats, or bullet-pointed business objectives. It's easier to trim all the ambiguous elements and focus on the details and facts, to keep the messy stuff out of the business talk. We don't like to say it might not work or that we have to take a step forward and we're just hoping this is the right one, or that our logic is sound even if the outcome may not be ideal. But that's actually good stuff that resonates with the messy side of humans—the emotional and psychological factors that drive us. It allows people to see ideas, not just marching orders.

But the responsibility to share the mess doesn't lie only with leaders. We each have to seek it out, embrace it, and find ways to navigate it.

I was working with a client once who had a large reorganization looming. I didn't have a part in it, but the CEO discussed her ideas and vision with me. I gave her the same recommendation I give to every client on the verge of a reorg: develop a rock-solid communication plan. Explain the why and the vision and the inspiration. Recognize all the feelings and fears that kick in when people hear, "We're restructuring." Develop the plan and then deliver these messages over and over again in a variety of ways. Make sure you are heard. Then remind people again of the why. Even when you think you have been heard, do it again.

The CEO assured me she had that solid plan. Fast-forward a few months to the rollout: it didn't go well. Some people quit, some people freaked out and created a multitude of backchannel conversations, and others got in touch with people outside the organization to make sense of the changes. Now, the thing that shocked me was this: people would rather quit and talk crap with their coworkers than try to make the mess better. Did the CEO make mistakes? Maybe. Ultimately the communication plan was far less layered than I had recommended. But, also, a lot of people within that company simply accepted the rules as they interpreted them and threw themselves into victimhood rather than asking the CEO questions that would have explained the big picture. They didn't understand the why, and now, they probably never will.

It's easier to accept that everything is futile and broken than to try to help. But someone has to be willing to say, "This is dumb and I want to make it better."

Work will change when we figure out how to productively fight against the status quo by leveraging individual personalities and unique characters and by including more people and perspectives in everything we do. Everything is messy and ambiguous and unpredictable: deal with it. Working like a Boss means stepping outside the norms to embrace our human side. It's learning to make just enough sense of the mess to see it as an opportunity, rather than an obstacle to complain about at the proverbial water cooler. Working like a Boss means taking that on. It means breaking through the crusty stuff and diving into the juicy stuff.

*The accepted work narratives keep so much
good stuff out of our workplaces.*

Ditch What We've Been Doing

To embrace the mess, we have to do things differently. We have to finally admit that things aren't as effective as people. We have to look outside the norms and traditions and beyond the boundaries of conformity. We have to welcome all the human stuff with arms wide open. Are you ready for that? It takes some guts, but that's what you have (or are willing to pretend you have) if you're reading this.

We have to push boundaries and break these unspoken rules. We have to stop being sheep and start being, well, us. Some of us (pointing to myself here) have never been able to fall in line. I never fit in at work, so I had no option other than embracing my own inner weirdo.

What I've realized while managing my own insecurities and weirdness is that it doesn't take much to be a weirdo at work. It just takes not fitting into the exact version of sameness that prevails in traditional work culture. I was outspoken even in entry-level roles, I offered to take on projects that were outside my skill level, and I proposed new ideas when no one asked (and probably didn't want me to). Weird, weird, and weird.

Some other ways that I'm weird? I like video games and technology, and musicals and theater. I am impatient and loud. I have a lot of ideas; some are good, but I'm not always interested in the follow-through needed to make them a reality. I value directness over passive-aggressiveness. I am fascinated by people *and* I am an introvert and generally stick to myself. I can read a room but sometimes decide to ignore what I'm sensing because I want to make a point on my terms. I fiercely protect my teams and colleagues even when they bug me. I hate wearing "work" clothes. I am proud but know I have a lot to learn. I question things that don't make sense to me.

I own my weird. I let people know what's coming. It might be jarring at first, but eventually, people have come to expect it and value it. I'm not sure if it's because I'm the boss (though that probably doesn't hurt) or that I'm loud enough to give them the distinct feeling they don't have an option (very true).

Weirdos don't toe the line and don't believe in the value of fitting in. They aren't necessarily rude, obnoxious agitators. More typically, they just don't buy into the idea that we need to all be alike; they might even believe it would be better if we weren't (guilty!).

My experiences have shown me that weird can work and, in fact, often does. Why? Because weird isn't actually all that weird. It's human, relatable, and more normal than sheep falling in line. The truth is, everyone is a weirdo if they aren't like us. You don't like cilantro? That's weird,

I love it. You hated my favorite movie? That's weird, it's fantastic. Do you like horses? You're weird. They smell.

All humans are weird. Maybe that means none of us are? Either way, the further we move past conformity, the more we'll see new ideas flourish. No one actually fits the mold that traditional professionalism promotes. Some people try, but the mold is like an average: it's the sum of a bunch of things without being any of those things exactly.[25] So be you.

I spent years thinking about *how* to be my weird self at work without punishment, so I understand why most people still feel that way. It's a cultural trap: we hold up some unique people as revolutionary, disruptive, or geniuses but punish others for what appear to be equally unique ways of contributing. Steve Jobs was a rebel in a good way for his perfectionism and particularity, but female leaders are mistrusted if they demonstrate strong subjective opinions.[26] White men, as is the

25 Todd Rose, "When U.S. Air Force Discovered the Flaw of Averages," *The Star*, January 16, 2016, https://www.thestar.com/news/insight/2016/01/16/when-us-air-force-discovered-the-flaw-of-averages.html.

26 See Emily Bazelon, "A Seat at the Head of the Table," *New York Times Magazine*, February 21, 2019, https://www.nytimes.com/interactive/2019/02/21/magazine/women-corporate-america.html, and Priya Fielding-Singh, Devon Magliozzi, and Swethaa Ballakrishnen, "Why Women Stay Out of the Spotlight at Work," Harvard Business Review, August 28, 2018, https://hbr.org/2018/08/sgc-8-28-why-women-stay-out-of-the-spotlight-at-work for examples.

case with so much in Western professional culture, are given far more latitude than other groups of people, which makes it even more important that we welcome our own human selves with open arms and encourage others to do the same. We have to add archetypes other than "nerdy weirdo" to our wall of weirdos. Everyone looks, sounds, acts, and identifies differently than everyone else. Period.

The greater the understanding we have among our teams and with the people around us, the easier it is to work. This is the power of teams that work well together: their familiarity and comfort help them work better than the sum of their parts (the individuals).[27] Susan is good at establishing order; give her the spreadsheet task. Kiara is really good at strategizing, so put her at the helm of assessing our product assortment and viability. Pria is excellent at rallying people; she should lead up the change messaging and onboarding. Our personalities make us effective at work, so why do we put so much into titles and skills when considering who does what? Yes, some basic skills or knowledge must be taken into account, but then what? It's our *selves* that differentiate us.

As work has moved faster, the demands on and requirements of how we participate at work have evolved. Of course, that is the focus of working like a Boss: using your personal power to make work better by being

27 Emily Stone, "Building Great Teams," Kellogg School of Management, https://insight. kellogg.northwestern.edu/building-leading-great-teams-research.

more you. We are all Bosses; we all have the ability and smarts for it. We just let a lot of shoulds and can'ts get in our way. Don't wait for work to happen to you. If you do, you're letting conformity win. Don't be a victim of the status quo; be a driver of *your* way.

The reality is that no one will be comfortable with us until we are comfortable with ourselves.

Cut through Conformity

After years of working with weirdos of all varieties and helping people adapt to a work culture that truly embraces individuality, I've seen some patterns in how to build weirdo-friendly spaces. It's a lot easier than it sounds, but we have to consider what it really means to create spaces and teams that feel welcoming to people. We have to be willing to be the one to step up first and set an example. We have to confront our own expectations and be willing to accept others. We start by putting ourselves out there. Here are a few tips for doing that.

Stop Judging Yourself

Judgment is killing us. We have to stop judging ourselves, judging others, judging customers and clients, judging people higher up and lower down in the company, and gossiping about our judgments. All that judging usually starts with us. Many of us are so critical of our own actions that we lose sight of the fact that generally, we're doing a fine job.

Your weirdness will be different than mine. And your colleagues' weirdnesses will be different from yours. That means we will all have to get more comfortable with variety rather than conformity—and that opens up a lot of opportunity for judgment. So let's just not. Let you be you and let Shane be Shane and Jessica be Jessica. If we don't, we are distracted from our actual jobs.

The change mindset we need to succeed in the business world in the twenty-first century is enabled by trust and acceptance in the workplace—of yourself and everyone around you. We have to redirect our energy from conforming and enforcing conformity to accepting, supporting, and harnessing all the ways people can be themselves. It means working to understand each other and working with that variety rather than against it.

While we probably can't quiet our judgy minds entirely, the judgments we bestow upon ourselves make it worse for other people too. By minimizing self-criticism, you will start to create a more welcoming energy. Just as judging ourselves manifests in judging others, being kind and compassionate with ourselves manifests in more kindness and compassion toward others.

The greatest thing we can do for others is to make space for them to be themselves. We shouldn't make people stay within a box, nor should we require them to share aspects of themselves that they do not want to. Let them be them.

Show Your Skin

I'm not talking about crop tops and short shorts. I'm talking about the skin you're in: you. If you haven't figured it out yet, the best way to work like a Boss is to figure yourself out and own it. Get comfortable with it. Ditch the drama of hiding your inner self or pretending you're something you're not. Own your weirdness, and embrace who you are.

Working well with others starts with self-awareness. *Work Like a Boss* focuses on individual action in part because, yes, we are the key to change, but also because our individual strengths are what will make it all possible. Here's a secret: no matter how weird your weirdest traits, thoughts, or habits are, you are not the only one with those weirdnesses. Someone else—in fact, I promise you, *lots* of someone elses—thinks the exact same way you do. And that can bring you together.

I encourage you to find one small release of your weirdness every week. Crack one small joke in a meeting—you might shift the energy of the room. Mention your niche hobby when you're meeting someone new— you might connect unexpectedly. These aren't huge reveals, and yet they can move you closer to the people around you.

The more comfortable you are in your skin, the more it changes who you are in business. When I finally started being more human at work, I realized that I could lift other people up, and others' weirdnesses could lift me up.

I became more patient because I wasn't trying to be things I'm not, so I wasn't worried about catching up with other people. I was just me.

When I finally embraced all my idiosyncrasies, I got so much better at my job and at being a good colleague. I used to feel bad that I didn't enjoy follow-through as much as ideation, but then I realized I partnered very well with a finisher. We complement each other, and that collaboration works well for both of us. My loudness and directness got me into uncomfortable situations at jobs early in my career, but people eventually came to trust and even look to me for that very candidness. I was never like the people around me, but I never wanted to pretend I was. That commitment to myself paid off when I met business partners who valued exactly what I brought. (Well, most of it.)

Talk about Inclusion

One theme throughout this book is the power of talk. There is danger in the unspoken and the things we shush. Putting intentional words to previously not-spoken-about things has power. Putting words and conversations to thoughts and feelings can jumpstart action. Just saying out loud "I want people to feel free to be themselves" can signal to people that you're open to seeing more of their authentic selves.

My company is relatively small. Over the years, we've had anywhere from twenty-five to one hundred people. There is no way I can improve the diversity of the workforce in our city, given how small we are, and yet I knew I wanted to make an impact. If I can't hire hundreds of thousands of people, what could I do? I could talk about diversity and how important it is. I could focus on inclusion and making the one space I could control—my company—a more inclusive environment. So I talked. I talked a lot and to whoever would listen.

I talked about as many layers of inclusion as I could, including how many people will mess up. When my colleague came to me to discuss the best way to handle a gender transition in the workplace setting, we talked about how people would—not might, would—mess up along the way. I would, she would, and our colleagues and clients would, whether it was saying something incorrect or not knowing the right words to respectfully engage about the topic of gender nonconformity. To me, it was crucial to acknowledge that going in. Partly it was selfish: I had known this person for years as a man and it would take time for me to retrain my brain. But also because fostering a truly inclusive space means making room for messing up. Making that space allowed us to transition with her in a much shorter time. Because we alleviated the fear of doing the wrong thing together, we all embraced her new identity and correlating pronouns in no time at all.

One of the reasons diversity and inclusion are so hard is because they require confronting ourselves.[28] Our fears, our identities, our limitations, our differences, and more are revealed, and with this comes feelings and reactions that are not always easy or comfortable. This confrontation goes against what we know, and most people are comfortable with conformity

---

28 Many, many things make diversity and inclusion difficult, including systemic racism, white supremacy, and centuries of inequity. I am not suggesting that this one element will make it all better. Within workplace interactions and relationships, this is what I've observed and heard about from peers.

and similarity. Speaking to the discomfort—the newness of navigating the unfamiliar—and admitting we will make mistakes along the way can go a long way toward improving the inclusiveness of a microenvironment.

While business has been shaped by the same kind of person for too long, business is never only *for* that same kind of person. Businesses produce goods and services that are *for everyone*—of all genders, races, religions, and flavors of weird. So it makes sense that when companies allow their weirdos to shape output, the products get better: more unique and more appealing.

Ask about Them

Humans have many interests, including a lot of nonwork things: family, music, food, movies, theater, travel, books, pets, plants, sports, and more. Duh, right? I did tell you I would just be reminding you of things you already knew! But the reality is that we sometimes ignore all these nonwork things while we're at work. We get so caught up in the reports and meetings that we don't dig beneath that office veneer. And there is so much value in it.

Be curious about what makes people tick. Ask what part of their job is their favorite or what part they find most challenging. Ask about their weekends and their hobbies. You will start to see layers beyond the mechanics of how they work. Offer your own stories about similar things. Give them opportunities to see you as broader and deeper than your own work self.

We gain so much insight by seeing more than a single facet of a person and by sharing more than a single facet about ourselves. It's incredible how much connection can happen in a few conversations. And the truth is, work is better when we enjoy the people around us.

Emotions are assets, not liabilities.

Show Your Emotional Side at Work

Emotions at work?! Yeah. In fact, hell yeah! They are already there, I promise. They are under the surface, between the cracks, and embedded in every comment, reaction, and interaction.

For decades, emotions have been cast as weak and weird, while calculating, dispassionate decision-making is perceived as rooted in strength and normalcy. We know from the fear chapter (and life in general) that emotions and cognition work hand in hand. And we know from experience that emotions are everywhere, all the time, whether we acknowledge them or not. We also know that when we ignore emotions, they don't go away. They just come out sideways, unpredictable or misdirected (that's part of the big mess I'm talking about here!). So what can we do? Embrace them.

In a study, doctors found that social sensitivity is a key factor in producing more and better outcomes when working with a team. Social sensitivity is "the personal ability to perceive and understand the feelings and viewpoints of others."[29] Essentially, it's emotional intelligence.

We've all done or said something that feels way more dramatic or aggressive than intended, so much that it catches us off guard. That's usually thanks to some kernel of an emotion that you shoved into a corner on time-out (you: *"I'll deal with you later!"*) that is now sick of it and ready to get out (your emotion: *"You'll deal with me when I want you to!"*).

As we bring more and more dimensions of ourselves to work, we will have to navigate those more individual and personal elements too. That might sound complicated, but the fact is, once we start dealing with all of this stuff more directly and explicitly, it will get easier. It's hard now because we don't do it a lot, and certainly not much in work scenarios.

I bring up emotional intelligence at work all the time because those soft skills (as they are often called) can be far more important than supposed

---

29 Anita Williams Woolley, Christopher F. Chabris, Alex Pentland, Nada Hashmi, and Thomas W. Malone, "Evidence for a Collective Intelligence Factor in the Performance of Human Groups," *Science* 29, no. 330, issue 6004 (October 2010): 686–88, https://science. sciencemag.org/content/330/6004/686.

hard skills—and, ironically, far more difficult. We spend so much time in school and jobs focused on our expertise that we forget that the mushy stuff is the glue that holds all the details together. In an article titled "New LinkedIn Research: Upskill Your Employees with the Skills Companies Need Most in 2020,"[30] LinkedIn added emotional intelligence to its list of top five soft skills. The article noted that all five skills—creativity, persuasion, collaboration, adaptability, and emotional intelligence—were more human-centered than those listed in previous years, which tended to be more task-oriented. This doesn't surprise me because as we progress further into the twenty-first century, there is more uncertainty and interdependence than ever in business and that requires distinctly human qualities.

Emotions are not weak. Emotions are strong and good—and necessary. There are other books that explain emotional strength and intelligence in more depth than what I can go into here, but the bottom line is that acknowledging and processing emotions in a responsible way, even in a business context, creates connections, leads to better solutions, and releases pressure.

---

30 Amanda Van Nuys, "New LinkedIn Research: Upskill Your Employees with the Skills Companies Need Most in 2020," LinkedIn, December 28, 2019, https://learning.linkedin.com/blog/learning-thought-leadership/most-in-demand-skills-2020.

EQ 101

Emotional intelligence starts with understanding yourself. (Here we go again with "It starts with you!" Are you picking up on a theme?) From a personal perspective, emotional intelligence is the ability to tap into and manage your own emotions. By being tuned in to what you're thinking and feeling, you can start to see how those internal aspects affect your behaviors out in the world and with people around you.

From an interpersonal perspective, emotional intelligence is about connecting with other people in appropriate ways and knowing your role in fostering a dynamic with them. This includes understanding human behavior and interactions; considering nonverbal cues, language, and nuance; and facilitating a healthy, productive exchange of energy and information. That's all. No biggie, right?

Flexing Emotional Intelligence

Emotional intelligence is a wildly underutilized tool in finding power at work. While I don't have the space to walk you through every detail of building it, I want to share some stuff that will kick yours into gear while on the clock.

Pay Attention to the Energy You Bring into a Room

Every time you engage with someone, you're not just exchanging words; there are layers of nonverbal communication going on, including eye contact, tone, and most importantly, energy. When you're pissed and in a terrible mood, or when you're in a great mood, it affects any conversation you have. Energy is contagious; sometimes that's a blessing and sometimes it's a curse. You don't have to be a chipper, cheery person every moment of the day (I'd be screwed if that was the case), but knowing where your mind and emotions are at gives you the power to enter interactions with more honesty.

Every Boss knows their energy can make or break a deal, a conversation, or a relationship. We've often learned it the hard way after high-stakes conversations went poorly or we inadvertently offended an innocent colleague. I've snapped at coworkers, only to have to apologize later and explain that my reaction wasn't about them but about something else on my mind. I've also been so distracted that I've derailed entire meetings. I am not too proud to own this, but I also know it's not a good pattern to establish.

Beyond the benefits of knowing when your energy might work against you, you can also use your awareness to make it work *for* you. Now we're talking, right? The real Boss move is to get your head around the outcome you want and align your energy with that. When your words and energy capture the energy you want from others, you can be more effective in conveying your point. Pay attention to whether you're in a negative place or a positive one, if you're in mindset to persuade or dissuade, and if you're putting out energy that attracts interest or repels it.

You can't control work, and you can't control other people. You can always control the energy you bring to a conversation. Always.

Listen and Watch as Much as You Talk

Understanding other people *and* how you affect them requires you to shut up and listen sometimes. Actually, a lot of the time. Emotional intelligence is only learned through interactions and observation.

When I'm in a meeting, I am rarely the loudest or the most talkative. It's not as effective as listening and watching to determine the most productive way to make my point. One of the boards I serve on is filled with professionals who are some of the best and brightest in their fields. They are smart and they know it, and most of them talk a lot at the meetings. I don't. Initially, it was due in part to my imposter syndrome (yes, we all have it), but after I settled in, I realized it wasn't useful for me to talk just for the sake of contributing. I listen, I wait, and I make a point when it's the right time. And I only know the right time by listening.

We often get so inside our heads or focused on what *we* think that we forget to look up and learn from what's going on around us. This is especially true at work. Can you think of a time when you've been in a conversation with someone, but while they were talking, you were thinking about how to reword your own point rather than thoughtfully listening? We've all done it. Humans are self-absorbed creatures. Sadly, we tend to focus even more on our inner thoughts when stakes or emotions are running high. We want to be right; we want to "win" the discussion. But those are short games. The long game is understanding people enough to work better *with* them, not against them.

Listening and watching give you insight into both how well you are making your point and what the other person's core interest is. Listening and watching allow you to absorb the other person's perspective and engage more meaningfully. Listening and watching help you figure out the nonverbal messages that are flying around a room. They are gold.

Lead with Curiosity, Not Criticism

We already covered the perils of judging too much, but actively leading with curiosity puts you in a position to truly empathize with others. Empathy is a buzzword in business right now, but that's because it works.[31] It grows genuine connections and expands our minds and perspectives.

---

31 Yoram Solomon, "Why Empathy Is the Most Important Skill You'll Ever Need to Succeed," *Inc.*, October 4, 2017, https://www.inc.com/yoram-solomon/10-reasons-empathy-is-most-important-business-skill-you-will-ever-need.html.

Good business requires a lot of perspectives. They help elevate new ideas and push things forward. But differing ideas can produce conflict and disagreements. Gasp! That's where curiosity is vital (and criticism a dead weight).

- If someone disagrees with you, ask them questions until you truly see their perspective. Make your goal understanding them, not changing their mind.

- If someone doesn't seem to be understanding your point, ask them what elements are not clear. Have them help you make your point better.

- Tap into emotions within a conversation by asking what people are hung up on, afraid of, or hope to achieve. By stepping back from making your points, you might learn how to make those points clearer and how to better communicate with the person.

The trick is to actually *be* curious. That's on you. (I can only do so much.) But you can't fake it. If you are trying to sound curious but actually being critical, it will backfire. Have the self-awareness to be curious. Have the self-awareness to know that your perspective isn't the only one and that others might have something to contribute. Also, just know that curiosity can help you make your point.

Use Your Words

Yep, I am back to that damn talking thing again. Why? Because we don't do it enough! Or, at least, not about the right things. We often don't talk about feelings, intuitions, new ideas, and so on because we don't know how. Bosses try, even when they aren't quite sure how to do it or how it will be received. Bosses are willing to be the people who forge new paths and carve out new patterns within their workplaces.

Even though much of emotional intelligence relies on nonverbal attributes, actually talking to people about what's going on is necessary. We shy away from this because we don't want to pry, or we don't think it's our business, or we just don't know what to say. I spend the entire next chapter on building communication skills, but here are a few ways to get better at using your words to build emotional intelligence at work.

- If you observe dynamics or body language, follow up with the people who displayed it. "I saw you look away when the boss brought up that client. What's going on there?" or "You've been really quiet in meetings recently. Is there anything I can do to help make space for you?"

- Your words can help build self-awareness. Ask your colleagues for feedback about your own behavior.

- Get therapy. Work out your dysfunction some place other than work and let your workmates reap the benefits of your efforts.

- Read therapy books and bring the concepts to work with you. Discuss books such as *Crucial Conversations: Tools for Talking When Stakes Are High* at work. Human psychology is everywhere, including work.

Words are powerful. Use them well, and use them thoughtfully. Emotions aren't a science, but they are very learnable. Individuals have personal patterns, and humans as a group have patterns. Pay attention, practice, and put your observations into action.

Dealing with the Emotionally Unintelligent

Unsurprisingly, not everyone has emotional intelligence. Even though you can't change them (other than buying them a copy of this book), you can still work with them productively.

The Steamroller—who ignores all common decency

Don't confront them in front of a group. If they don't care about being diplomatic or sensitive under normal conditions, they will not respond respectfully if called out. Have a one-on-one conversation with them and practice the skills above. Be curious, ask questions, and help them understand how their behavior affects the group. Lead with empathy, not assumptions about why this person acts the way they do.

The Clueless—who just has no idea how their actions or words affect others

The Clueless differs from the Steamroller in that their behavior is not necessarily intentional; they just aren't paying attention. When I think of my own industry, I think of the software engineer stereotype; in other industries, a similar stereotype is applied to accountants. "They just don't get it." Emotional intelligence is hard to teach, but having a conversation with the Clueless about what you're seeing might help them become a little more aware. Ask what they notice about the emotional dynamics of the group to see if they are picking up on more than you might be aware of. Share your experience of their lack of emotional awareness and how it shapes your work with them.

The Overemotional—who shares everything
or dwells too much on all the soft stuff

Sometimes too much is too much, and you, personally, have to put emotions aside and get to work. You can refocus on work while not being dismissive of people who take longer to process or appear caught up on emotional aspects of work. I have two strategies for the Overemotional: refocus their attention on the common goal or give them permission to take space if they need it. They will assess their mindset and determine whether they have the ability to move forward in that moment or need more time. I have found that it's best to encourage people to move through emotions rather than ignore them. Ignoring them tends to slow people down and let emotion fester. At Clockwork, we have a small room dedicated to emotional breaks. It a cozy space with an armchair and sofa that comforts and relaxes people. People use it for a variety of reasons (including napping, and that's fine with me), but usually it's just a place to calm one's mind and center. Let people take the time they need. You can keep going and catch them up.

The Heart-on-the-Sleeve—who shows every thought on their face

These are the colleagues who can't seem to hide stress, fear, anger, and all the other emotions we go through each day. If they are stressed, you will be too after you spend five minutes with them. I usually talk to these colleagues privately about their impact. They rarely intend to be that transparent about their emotions or thoughts, but they often need reminders to keep their internal selves in check. I often explain that looks—versus words—put a lot of emotional labor on others. They wonder what's wrong, whether they should ask you about it, and if it's about them. That's not an appropriate pattern to develop with coworkers. An "I want to throw up" look on someone's face is far more terrifying (and mystifying) than being told directly, "I am very nervous about my client presentation next hour." *That* you can work with, but a frozen face you can't.

The common thread here? Talk to people openly but privately. Not only will it make work better, but you will also start developing new discussion and feedback skills that will continue to serve you. If this sounds like a lot of effort, I say, "Welcome to the actual work of work!"

Let Freak Flags Fly

So you've started to chip away at conformity and paid a little more attention to your emotional intelligence at the office. The last step to embracing the messiness of work is creating the space for *everyone* to embrace it by centering your work environment on humans. Just put the human side of business right in the middle of things. The messiness, the weirdos, the idiosyncrasies, the honest truths about people. If you're able to shift only a small slice of your general workplace pie, that's a great start.

Believe it or not, focusing on the people around you at work is much easier than trying to work around them. And not just letting but *encouraging* people to be themselves is also easier.

Since we can't avoid people, commit to making it all about them. It makes each day go faster, it makes problems less difficult to solve, and it makes you smarter because you're constantly learning how to interpret and adapt to the environment around you. And creating space that encourages others to do the same helps you even more. Empowering others empowers you. And that's when you find your power.

This was something my business partners and I were very intentional about from the start because we truly believe—and have shown with our company—that if we make work as conducive as possible to the human side of business, we get better outcomes. I read somewhere that happy people do good work. Based on our experiences and our personal values, we knew that if people didn't have to "behave" in all the ways we've discussed so far, we'd save ourselves and our colleagues a lot of energy. And we'd all enjoy ourselves much more along the way. Now, you're probably not building a company from the ground up (if you are, give me a call—I have a lot of advice), but you do want to make shit better.

Centering your approach to work on other people doesn't mean you have to enjoy them or want to hang out with them outside of work, or that you have to be a people person at all. You just have to accept and understand them and get your ego out of the way. Easy, right?! Ha. I know.

Once our emotions, our differences, our honesty, our fears, and our selves are out on the table, we can start to build trust and achieve a level of openness that allows true collaboration and partnership.

The (Psychological) Safety Dance

In its now-famous Aristotle Project, Google discovered that the key to high-performing teams wasn't individual knowledge or even hard work. It was how safe the team members felt working together.[32] These findings were not new, though the project seems to be one of the first times the concept of psychological safety was applied to technology teams.

Remember when we talked in the fear chapter about our reptilian responses to perceived threats? A challenging question from a boss or a provocation from a colleague can feel like a threat to parts of our brain, triggering emotional responses in the amygdala that don't align with the

---

32 Charles Duhigg, "What Google Learned From Its Quest to Build the Perfect Team," *New York Times Magazine*, February 25, 2016, https://www.nytimes.com/2016/02/28/magazine/what-google-learned-from-its-quest-to-build-the-perfect-team.html.

actual threat. This happens at work all the time when tense or uncomfortable topics are on the table. Psychologist Laura Delizonna explains, "The amygdala, the alarm bell in the brain, ignites the fight-or-flight response, hijacking higher brain centers. This 'act first, think later' brain structure shuts down perspective and analytical reasoning. Quite literally, just when we need it most, we lose our minds. While that fight-or-flight reaction may save us in life-or-death situations, it handicaps the strategic thinking needed in today's workplace."[33] This general stupidity of our brains is why psychological safety has become an important factor in workplaces that require people to work together (i.e., every job ever from now on).

Amy Edmonson, who has studied psychological safety for decades and originated the concept,[34] defines it in her TEDx talk as "a belief that one will not be punished or humiliated for speaking up with ideas, questions, concerns, or mistakes."[35] In an interview, Edmonson also notes,

33 Laura Delizonna, "High-Performing Teams Need Psychological Safety. Here's How to Create It," *Harvard Business Review*, August 24, 2017, https://hbr.org/2017/08/high-performing-teams-need-psychological-safety-heres-how-to-create-it.

34 Amy Edmondson, "Psychological Safety and Learning Behavior in Work Teams," *Administrative Science Quarterly* 44, no. 2 (June 1999): 350–83, https://www.jstor.org/stable/2666999.

35 Amy Edmondson, "Building a Psychologically Safe Workplace," TEDxHGSE talk, May

"Psychological safety isn't about being nice. It's about giving candid feedback, openly admitting mistakes, and learning from each other."[36] I am particularly drawn to this comment because it illuminates a more realistic picture. Candid feedback and commentary require comfort with directness; openly admitting mistakes means acknowledging failures; learning from each other requires collaboration and a desire for equity among colleagues.

From my experience in offices and working with clients, building a safe environment of this kind means ridding workplaces of some very common elements: passive-aggressiveness, rigid hierarchy, ego-driven power trips, fiefdoms, territorialism, and "niceness."

The attributes that we need to exhibit at work now—risk taking, problem solving, experimentation—can be very scary to our brains. They require us to work closely with other people who will likely push our buttons, question us, and behave irrationally at times. These psychological safety studies show us that we must work against our brains and against our instincts. Edmondson makes additional points that "the reason why psychological safety is rare has to do with aspects of human

---

4, 2014, https://www.youtube.com/watch?v=LhoLuui9gX8.

36 Amy Edmondson, "Creating Psychological Safety in the Workplace," *Harvard Business Review*, January 22, 2019, https://hbr.org/ideacast/2019/01/creating-psychological-safety-in-the-workplace.

nature, human instinct. You know, for example, it is an instinct to want to look good in front of others. It's an instinct to divert blame, you know it's an instinct to agree with the boss. And hierarchies are places where these instincts are even more exaggerated. We really want to look good and we especially want to look good in a hierarchy."

Studies show that we hate losing more than we like winning, and admitting we failed at something feels an awful lot like losing, so we don't speak up. We want to play it safe, so we don't give candid feedback. We want to feel special, so we hoard information.

I know there are workplaces where real safety is an issue, where people feel genuinely afraid to raise flags or contribute new ideas. I also know that some people experience different barriers to feeling safe at work. I can't fix all that, as much as I wish I could.

Sowing Safety

Despite psychological safety going against our evolutionary instincts and much of our learned behavior, it's not actually that complicated to cultivate. To me, the steps are mostly about ridding yourself and your environment of some bad habits. So what are we to do?

In her TED Talk, Edmonson outlines three steps each individual can personally take to bring more psychological safety to our teams:

1. Frame the work as a learning problem, not an execution problem.
2. Acknowledge your own fallibility.
3. Model curiosity and ask lots of questions.

These are fantastic recommendations. Through personal experience, I've discovered a few other ways to chip away at the barriers that prevent safe environments at work.

Stop Judging

Yes, I gave this advice just a few pages back, and yes, I am going to give it again. I can't give it enough. If we stopped judging ourselves and others so harshly, we would A) have a lot more time to think about productive things, and B) realize that it's a complete waste of time. If there is judgment, there can't be safety. Period.

In *Daybook: The Journal of an Artist*, the artist Anne Truitt wrote something that spoke to me about the danger of judgment and the benefits that we can experience if we refrain from it.

Unless we are very, very careful, we doom each other by holding onto images of one another based on preconceptions that are in turn based on indifference to what is other than ourselves. We claim autonomy for ourselves and forget that in so doing we can fall into the tyranny of defining other people as we would like them to be. By focusing on what we choose to acknowledge in them, we impose an insidious control on them. I notice that I have to pay careful attention in order to listen to others with an openness that allows them to be as they are, or as they think themselves to be. The shutters of my mind habitually flip open and click shut, and these little snaps form into patterns I arrange for myself. The opposite of this inattention . . . is the honoring of others in a way that grants them the grace of their own autonomy and allows mutual discovery.

Mutual discovery. What a brave concept at work: to position your mind and self to be open to discovery, learning, and sharing. It sounds a little cheesy, but it's a much better use of your time and energy than judgment or exclusion.

Create Team Values or a Shared Code of Conduct
Articulating shared targets can inspire conversations about behaviors, communication styles, and what you and your colleagues are willing to commit to together. It elevates and makes very obvious the values you all stand behind. It also establishes a record you can point to if an individual strays from that agreement.

Even writing a personal code of conduct and sharing it with others can inspire safety and let others know how *you* feel about openness and acceptance. By establishing that with peers, you create a microclimate that can have a big impact.

Talk about Safety

Repeating your personal, cultural, or organizational commitment to safety is a must. A common truism states you have to say something seven times for people to remember it. And that's just to remember, not to actually *feel* and *believe*. In my experience, that takes another seven thousand repetitions. Humans are hardwired to believe what they've experienced, and sadly, few of us have experienced safety among colleagues. Many of us might not have experienced acceptance or safety anywhere.

Focus on Outcomes, Not Outputs

Our culture is very tied to outputs—how much we do, what we own, what we earn—which is probably a holdover from our production-oriented industries. It's all quantity over quality. By making space for other symbols or measurements of success, we create more pathways for understanding our work. An outcome doesn't have to be something tangible: it can be a lesson learned, a mistake made, or a relationship strengthened.

To focus on outcomes instead of outputs, ask, "What did you learn?" instead of "What did you accomplish?" Ask, "What will we do differently next time?" rather than "What went wrong?" Focus team discussion on lessons as much as results. Talk to people about their contributions and learn from their opinions of their part in the whole. Help people around you focus on how they can do better next time, not how they failed this time.

Don't Focus on Negativity

This is another repeat recommendation, and that's intentional. Negativity is so, so easy. It's our default, but it's not going to help anyone feel safe. Negativity makes us walk on eggshells; it makes us nervous and fearful. Failures and mistakes will happen at work, so how do we generate a space that doesn't spiral out of control when they do? How do we train our personal and team reflexes to get interested in failure and mistakes as growth opportunities?

Sidestep the Blame Game

Yep, we could all devote endless time to figuring out who to blame. Or, how about we skip that step and focus on how to make it better? It's tempting to find out "whodunnit," but at work, the results of that quest don't *really* move anything forward other than our selfish curiosity. Better questions to ask when something goes wrong are:

- Is there something about the process we should change?

- How can we continually improve?
- What could we implement that would help us ensure this issue doesn't happen again?

Basically, don't be mean when something implodes. Find a solution instead.

At times, you might be exercising these steps just by yourself and with yourself. That's okay. Creating a safe environment for yourself is an important first step.

I think I first set out to find or create psychological safety at work because I am gay. The first time I felt safe was when I was in college, majoring in theater. By nature, theater has to be a safe place: it requires vulnerability, risks, and emotions. Oftentimes, the most extraordinary ideas in theater are not obvious ideas. There is risk in trying new things and imagining what could be instead of just reflecting what has always been. When I was there, with those peers, I could just be me. I could contribute everything I had to offer and help make great things—often out-of-the-box ideas. I hadn't had that anywhere else, and I thrived.

I didn't end up in theater (although sales feels awfully close some-times), but I did spend my entire career trying to replicate the feelings I had during those few years. I started working thirty years ago, when being gay wasn't welcomed in the workplace or accepted by people around me. It wasn't something I could wear on my sleeve. For years I shut down that part of me in all parts of my life and most especially at work. Even after I accepted and embraced who I was outside of work, I still carried a shield at the office. I don't want that for anyone, inside or outside of Clockwork, so I started doing whatever I could, whenever I could, to create more safety.

One of the highest achievements of my career happened when my colleague came to me and said that, for the first time in their life, their personal and professional lives had aligned in such a way that they realized they identified as a different gender than what they were assigned at birth. We discussed why, and a big part of their realization happened because they felt safe enough to explore dimensions of themselves that they hadn't felt open to before. Being in a genuinely safe environment changed their own perspective on themself. This was an important moment for me because it showed that safety and acceptance could transform people. Work matters in the context of a person's whole life.

The safety of humans is sacred to me. We were trying to create a safe place at Clockwork, and my colleague showed me that they actually *felt* safe. When people feel safe, they can be themselves, they can perform at their optimal level, they bring radical ideas to projects, and they are more likely to perpetuate safety around them. When we all feel safe with each other, we create stronger bonds with people—think of "foxhole friends," the ones who make you feel safe even if everything around you is going off the rails. That is possible only when we strive to make ourselves and our workplace safe.

Work Like a Boss Takeaways

1. Being you, yourself, your whole self, and nothing but yourself is not only smart and effective but also productive.
2. Spend time developing emotional intelligence to make the best of your relationships and projects.
3. Expand your awareness and cultivation of psychological safety to create healthy spaces that let everyone—yourself and others—be who they are in order to contribute the fullest.

Chapter Six

TALK LIKE A HUMAN

In the late 1990s, I worked on a project that changed the trajectory of my career. I was working at Bitstream Underground, an early internet service provider in the Twin Cities, and our client, a Midwestern leader in their field, hired us to build a new website that united several divisions of their company under a holistic, streamlined web experience. I had previously been in marketing, communications, PR, and media, but had found my true calling—technology—when I started working at Bitstream and applied all my production knowledge to internet experiences. I worked my way up and around (including sales, customer support, and driving to people's houses with a floppy disk to install software), and by the late 1990s I was president. I was a regular Mary Tyler Moore in pants and nerdy glasses. I was making things happen. I was strategic. I kind of knew what I was talking about. I felt awesome.

Then this project happened. Well, really, I should say that a particular person happened. At that time, it was a big job and I was excited to be working on it. We were a reputable company and brought a great mix of backgrounds to our client's projects, including creative, communications, technology, and sales. My colleagues were whip-smart and super pro. Because I came up through the ranks of project management, I was often integrally involved in day-to-day client work. That was the case with this project, and I was privy to all the communication between our team and the client's project manager. The latter, however, was difficult— really, really difficult. She was condescending, rude, belligerent, and demanding. She talked to us like we were the dumbest people alive. She would make decisions that changed the scope of the project and then wouldn't take responsibility for them. She treated me, in particular, in crappy ways. It became clear that she didn't think we had the ability to manage a large project effectively, so I knew that we had to do one thing well: manage the project effectively. I put everything I could into it and quickly made up a process and a chain of communication that would serve us well in the face of a difficult person.

At the end of the project, I found myself in a room with the client's boss and several other executives. They were trying to blame us for all the pain and hardship throughout the project. What saved me was a folder full of printouts of every single email we ever sent on the project. I'll never forget it because the folder was as tall as a pencil and very impressive. With it, I was able to point to the approvals and decisions that the client's project manager had made.

In hashing out the details and failings of the project, I realized that their communication was ineffective in part because it was passive-aggressive. It was demoralizing and diminishing, and not direct. It was about blame and shame instead of shared responsibility and healthy collaboration.

What I got from that experience was an initial sense of how to work with people. I understood that a team's communication style dramatically affected the outcomes it achieved. That's when I started to outline what I valued about partnerships and how to implement those values: open communication, mutual respect, and covering your ass. I realized how subjective and flimsy words and conversations are, so I adopted documentation, meeting recaps, and verbal directness at the expense of everything else. It's just too painful otherwise. I took that difficult project with me into everything I did after that.

A few years ago, I ran into that project manager at an event. She didn't remember me at all, and at the time I couldn't place her face or name. It wasn't until I was in an elevator later that day, thinking about something else entirely, that it dawned on me. *That's* who she was. Too bad it was too late to tell her that my entire first book, how I approach leadership, and my dedication to open communication can be traced back to that shitty experience.

What we learn and what is effective are at odds with each other.

The Complexity of Communication

If there is one thing I've learned from all these years of putting my metaphorical foot in my mouth, from watching people try and fail and try again and succeed, from challenging people to *say* what they mean, and from sitting in meeting after meeting after meeting, it's this: good communication is hard but possible. But only if:

- you own it (there's that damn accountability again),

- you don't let fear get in your way (crap, that fear thing again),

- and you really consider how you affect others (that "we're all weirdos, just embrace it" chapter isn't going anywhere either).

But the number-one thing that makes communication at work better? More. More is actually more. More direct, more empathetic . . . more human. We tend to be so consumed by our own experiences that we never consider how our communication might be received, what additional information other people need, or how people feel about what's being said. We focus on the message itself, but it's all the stuff around a message that determines how and if that message lands well.

Communication is hard. And yet, we're constantly doing it. A *Harvard Business Review* article from 2016 points out that in many companies, the average employee spends 80 percent of their time at work communicating.[37] Emails, meetings, phone calls can take up four-fifths of your day. Two things about this: 1) that's a *lot* of time, and 2) we'd better get good at it if we spend that much time doing it. But we aren't. Why?

We Don't Learn How to Do It

No one teaches us how to communicate, especially not how to do it in a work setting. We are lucky if we get useful lessons out in the world, but, generally, our communication skills are informed by a mélange of experiences from school, our families, and the assortment of largely ir-relevant norms held over from decades of work culture.

We do learn a bit about communication in high school and col-lege, but it's primarily one-directional: how to write a paper or make a compelling argument. All through school, communication as a skill is ignored because we know how to talk and write, right? Boom! That's

---

37 Rob Cross, Reb Rebele, and Adam Grant, "Collaborative Overload," *Harvard Business Review* (January–February 2016), https://hbr.org/2016/01/collaborative-overload.

communication! So we all participate in an unconscious assumption that we all know how to communicate. But we often don't know how to do it well. At work, we need to engage, not just present. We need to understand what other people are saying even when it's a stretch for us to do so. We need to know whether they understand us, even when they won't say so one way or the other. Communication isn't unidirectional. It is bidirectional, multidirectional, and collaborative at work (and ideally everywhere). We need to find ways to actually work *together* and build on, not just share, ideas.

We learn the majority of our communication skills from our families of origin. How our parents gave feedback is how we likely do it, and how they responded is likely how we do too. How our parents communicated with each other and with us is the primary influence on our own ability to communicate. That's a little scary, right? Most families aren't terrible, but more often than not, family politics create homes that, like offices, are petri dishes for unhealthy communication. While my mother was a great role model for me as a businessperson, we had tough times talking directly about anything outside of her professional sphere—so, you know, most things.

What we "know" about communication at work has been informed by outdated corporate machines. As we've already discussed, they are largely dysfunctional, and yet people keep doing what the machine has always done. Nothing gets addressed or fixed.

Nothing highlights this dysfunction as much as the conflict between our twenty-first-century digital behaviors and our twentieth-century norms. Digital technology changed how we behave in the world everywhere, not just at work. It has democratized who gets to share their voice and story, it's leveled hierarchy, and it's given individuals unprecedented access to information. But when we show up to work, so many deeply entrenched job norms and expectations haven't caught up to these behaviors. People get assessed on their performance but don't have the opportunity to assess their managers. You have to be at the right table at the right time to share your ideas. Only some people get to know business-critical information, yet all people are expected to contribute their butts off. We aren't supposed to mention personal, political, or social stuff after 9:00 a.m., even though many colleagues might have already heard you share that exact stuff on Twitter or Facebook, or in the breakroom, and know that it's going to affect your day. The norms don't necessarily make sense anymore, but they're woven into the fabric of what we consider "professional" and in our collective way of doing things.

At work, how we can communicate has changed dramatically, but all our skills, expectations, and habits haven't. What does that leave us with

as we muddle through meetings and work partnerships? Various bits of family baggage and decades of "traditions" that feel foreign, and yet habitual, to us. What we learned and what is effective are at odds with each other.

Until now. We are going to unlearn and relearn. Right now.

We're Terrified

Fear is often the thing keeping us from being effective communicators. Remember the five types of fear from chapter 4? Here they again:

1. We fear conflict.
2. We're afraid we're not good enough.
3. We fear what others will think of us.
4. We fear we'll do the wrong thing.
5. We fear the unknown or unfamiliar.

I'm sure you can already see how these feed into bad communication habits. Much of what we have to tell others at work could feel like conflict: "I disagree with your conclusion" or "I think we should try something different." We fear that we might not be good at talking something through and let that fear keep us from trying—and from getting better by trying. We worry what other people will think of us if we bring up tough topics: Will my client still like me? Will my colleague think I'm too direct or overstepping my bounds? Fear of doing the wrong thing keeps us from doing anything. Moreover, the "wrong" thing isn't always actually wrong; it might just be unpopular or hard. Lastly, the unfamiliar and unknown keep our mouths shut. We don't know what will happen if we speak up, voice our opinion or displeasure, or reach out to someone and try to have an honest, two-way conversation. All these fears short-circuit our best intentions and disrupt our efficacy.

Some of the biggest risks we can and should take at work happen through communication. It is how we literally engage with people but also the metaphorical connective tissue. It closes gaps between people, between ideas and execution, and between differing opinions. All the elements of psychological safety require an ability to effectively communicate.

> *Communication is the lifeline and*
> *throughline of healthy workplaces.*

We Are Pros at Passive-Aggression

Passive-aggression might be my biggest pet peeve. I don't know if it's because I live in the Midwest, but I see, hear, and feel it all the time.

It's in meetings with clients, it's in boardrooms, it's in meetings with colleagues, it's on our phone calls with spouses (well, not mine, because she's a therapist and would call me out on that in a heartbeat). "Per my last email" is really someone saying, "I already asked you about this; why haven't you answered it?" at best, but probably more like, "Can you respond to my damn email?"

One official definition of passive-aggression reads, "a type of behavior or personality characterized by indirect resistance to the demands of others and an avoidance of direct confrontation."[38] Another: "a deliberate and masked way of expressing hidden anger."[39] A third describes a passive-aggressive person as one who "doesn't express negative feelings directly."[40] Lastly, it's "a pattern of indirectly expressing negative feelings instead of openly addressing them."[41] You can see the picture these are painting: saying or feeling one way and thinking or doing something totally different.

Passive-aggression is everywhere, and I think we might be so used to

---

38 https://www.lexico.com/en/definition/passive-aggressive

39 https://www.psychologytoday.com/us/blog/passive-aggressive-diaries/201704/why-passive-aggressive-behavior-thrives-in-the-workplace

40 https://www.webmd.com/mental-health/passive-aggressive-behavior-overview#1

41 https://www.mayoclinic.org/healthy-lifestyle/adult-health/expert-answers/passive-aggressive-behavior/faq-20057901

it at work that we aren't aware of it. But it eats away at productivity and morale. Whether you're the source of passive-aggressive behavior or the witness or victim of it, it is stealing and sabotaging your power because it's so insistent and yet hidden. It is draining us. And it's a complete waste of time.

We're taught from a very young age to be nice and to behave. Combine that with our outdated corporate norms (which are also tied to being nice and behaving) and spending the majority of our waking hours in a hamster cage with people we didn't choose, and you have a recipe for implosion! The result is that we spend hours at work stewing and complaining about what's wrong or sidestepping problems because we don't want to rock the boat. Whatever we do, it certainly isn't addressing what's wrong head-on. Where's the fun in that?

As I was writing this book, I put a call out for stories of passive-aggression at work. Some of the stories people shared were too cruel to repeat, but here's one of many examples of the ways people use passive-aggression instead of just talking to a person. "A creative director on a project didn't want to co-lead with me, he wanted to be the only one in charge. So he had the project manager cancel the project kickoff on ONLY my calendar. I assumed that it was canceled for everyone and was being rescheduled until I happened to WALK BY THE MEETING as it was in progress and see him holding court. So I stuck my head in there to ask what was going on and he had the nerve to tell me that he thought the meeting should only include the 'necessary' resources."

In just that one story, we have many attributes of passive-aggression: going behind someone's back instead of addressing them face-to-face, withholding information, and embarrassing someone in front of colleagues.

In another story, a friend shared this:

> I was a VP at a company with responsibility for operations, legal matters, and building new locations. The bank's president, who had hired and mentored me, left, and his successor really disliked me. One day, I went out to lunch and when I returned one of the drawers in my credenza was empty. He had someone take all of the important corporate files that I was responsible for in my role and put them in his office to be kept in a locked drawer. That's how I got the message that my future there was not rosy. He never spoke to me about those files, my performance, or my job.

A company president did that! This happens at all ranks of an organization and with all types of roles. Crappy communication at work is, unfortunately, universal.

In chapter 1, I included a list of common passive-aggressive behaviors at work. Here's a refresh:

- Chronically "forgetting" deadlines or "misplacing" important documents

- Procrastinating or carrying out tasks inefficiently

- Choosing not to take action that could prevent a problem from occurring

- Withholding important information

- Complaining endlessly and blaming others (often authority figures) for problems

- Undermining the authority of others through rumor, gossip, complaints, and innuendo

- Embarrassing coworkers in public settings such as meetings or presentations

- Using notes, voice mails, or electronic communications to avoid face-to-face confrontation

- Withdrawing and sulking rather than stating opinions or needs

- Using words like *fine* and *whatever* to shut down a discussion

- Giving lip service to doing things differently in the future while not planning to change the behavior

Passive-aggression is a big topic that encompasses many of the themes in this book, but I intentionally put it in the communication chapter. I think it's rampant because humans are not naturally effective communicators. We have all these feelings at work and can't figure out how to express them, so they come out sideways. In the story above, the creative director had a feeling about leading that he couldn't or didn't want to deal with directly. Maybe he was intimidated by his colleague, maybe he felt insecure about his collaboration skills, or maybe he really wanted a win at work because he was afraid of losing his job. Maybe it was none of those. Whatever his internal motivation, he chose to do that shitty thing and treat someone badly rather than try to communicate in a normal human way.

One of the reasons people participate in passive-aggressive behavior at work is that they have something they want another person to do or recognize, but they won't say it; they want the other person to just figure it out. They will talk around it but never say it outright. This is uncomfortable for both parties, especially the recipient. The message intended by "Per my last email" could easily be written, "Could you respond by

2:00 p.m.? I would love to bring that information to a meeting to help things get back on track."

What do we do? To reclaim power from passive-aggression we have to get direct, get specific, and get thoughtful. We have to ditch "nice" and "well-behaved" and find new qualities that define the right way to show up at work.

- Practice being direct: not rude or cruel, but saying what you mean.

- Remain cool, calm, and collected. Rather than letting all your emotions out sideways, point them straight ahead.

- Don't react at all. Just Do. Your. Work.

Good communication will take down passive-aggression because passive-aggression thrives when we let things go, when we're too concerned about being liked to be direct and clear in both words and actions. I'm here to say you can have both—you can communicate well *and* have solid relationships at home and at work. In fact, if you master healthy communication, you might just master relationships. Then you can write your own book. Do that.

Basics of Good Communication

I'm not going to pretend that this is the holy grail of all communication. This chapter is really just the tip of the iceberg. But there are some basics we forget when we think too much about *what* we need to say and less about *how* we're saying it. On the flip side, when we're receiving a message, we often focus on only a fraction of what's happening in the conversation instead of participating openly and fully.

No matter what you're saying or hearing, or how you're engaging with others, these four things should always be front of mind.

Context

Bad news, good news, and new ideas all need context. Context is king (or queen) and it will help you in every single conversation. Context is your friend. Context gives our emotions the grounding to settle down and gives us time to relax. Context provides information and diffuses the power imbalance between the person *with* the information and the

CONTEXTUALIZED MESSAGES

one without. Context helps get two people to a shared understanding. (Note that I didn't say *agreement*. It's not magic!)

At Clockwork, we call messages with no context "truth bombs." And that's how those messages *feel*, like tiny explosions that disrupt your world. In my line of business, we have to talk about difficult things all the time. As most people who work with clients know, clients want everything on their required list *and* their nice-to-have list, fast and cheap. Hell, when I'm a client I want the same thing! Don't we all? Because, wow, that sounds nice. But it's rarely possible, and that sucks to hear and sucks to say.

A truth bomb is calling a client and saying, "We're not going to be able to hit that deadline we set. We have to push it back four weeks. Okay?" Now, prior to this call, the client was likely doing something unrelated to the deadline. If they were thinking about it, it was within an entirely different context. So the call and the message come out of the blue. This is when context can help each person. The caller with the bad news has the opportunity to give the *why* and maybe even provide a middle-ground solution. Let's reimagine the call above: "Hi, Keisha. The team and I have realized the deadline we collectively set is at risk. Can I fill you in on the details and what we're hoping to do?"

There is a lot of space on the communication continuum between a giant truth bomb and a well-contextualized message. Most of us deliver messages somewhere in between. Here are a few questions to ask yourself before making those tough calls. Add whatever answers make sense for your relationship and the message.

- What do you know that the other person might not?
- What factors led to you sharing the message?
- Why do you think the idea/conclusion/outcome is okay?
- What does the person have to do with the information and how quickly?
- What is the person likely to feel in response to your news?

Acknowledge that last question from the start. If I'm going to deliver crappy news, I like to say, "I'm about to say something that's not going to feel great. But hear me out and let's talk through a solution." That is *always* my secret. Then speak to the goal: "We will be better for it. We will develop more trust and more transparency between us and find ways to work better. If I don't share it, you won't get better." I let them know what's coming and how I relate to what they're feeling about it.

If you're receiving a message and feeling like you don't have all the context you need, ask! I know we all hate to "look dumb" or "challenge other people," but it will help you—and them—get better at engaging. Here are a few options:

- I understand what you're saying, but can you talk me through your thought process?

- What are all the possible options aside from the one you recommend? I think that will help me see a fuller picture.

- What could have prevented this from happening?

- What do you need from me and when?

Intention

Know *why* you're saying what you're saying. Going into a conversation unclear on what you intend to communicate is a shortcut to a crappy conversation. In the client call above, the intention of the first (crappy) example seemed to be getting approval. In the second, more contextualized example, the intention was to help the client understand the situation. It's not a major difference, but just a slight tweak to how you deliver a message can change its reception dramatically.

Intention can make a difficult thing easier to say because, ideally, the reason you're saying it is positive. Difficult messages can be helpful, useful, or productive, but only when your intention is positive. If you're saying something just to be a dick or hurt someone's self-esteem, well, A) don't say it, and B) maybe go to therapy?

When you're on the receiving end of a message, keeping the other person's likely intention in mind can help you both stay productive. I say *likely* because you might not always know and you can't always get it out of them. But if you can, take a few seconds to step back and ask yourself, "Where is this person coming from with this message? Is it their intention to be helpful?" Sometimes in workplaces the intention isn't positive or good (two words: passive-aggression). But sometimes the intention *is* good but the execution is awkward or harsh or curt. It happens—in fact, I think this is usually the case! Good intentions, poor implementation. But that doesn't mean it has to devolve into crap. As one of the people in the conversation, you have the opportunity to respond to the intention (or the hopeful intention) in a way that corrects the course.

There has been a lot of talk recently about distinguishing between intention and impact. We can have a good intention *and* a shitty impact. I can intend for you to feel included and heard, and you could feel tokenized and called out. Pay attention—maybe even ask!—if you're making a very different impact than you intend. It suggests that there is a gulf between what you're thinking and feeling and how you're talking or doing.

Empathy

You know that sales saying, "Always be closing"? I say, "Always be empathizing." Always. Go into every conversation, every engagement, and every interaction thinking about the other person. Think about their emotions, their situation, their fears, their insecurities, their context. Of course, you won't know all this all the time, but you can imagine. If you're working in sales, perhaps that rude customer was up all night with a sick parent. If you're in an office, maybe that guy who talks down to you all the time is really insecure about his expertise.

Is the person a new parent? Maybe they're tired. How long have they been in their current role? Maybe they are nervous about performing well. Is their department going through turmoil? Maybe they are scared they will be laid off. How much do they know about you? Maybe they are just projecting their crap onto you. Think of this as the subtext—the stuff that's not being said but is still there, under the surface.

There is a lot of power in meeting someone where they are. There is a lot of power in allowing people to be who they are. There is also a lot of power in turning to empathy when people are being rude, mean, or difficult. There is power in leading with understanding even though the other person might not be doing the same. Being empathetic doesn't mean you take on whatever the person is thinking, feeling, or worrying about. It just means acknowledging those things to be true and adapting your approach if you need or want to. This is true for whichever role you're in during a conversation. Thinking about the other person shifts you from being defensive and makes you more open to honest engagement.

In the end, leading with empathy makes things easier for you. Yes, that's a bit of a selfish reason to put others first, but it's true and real. If someone at work is being short with me, I could imagine all the ways I'd like to tell them to screw off, or I could think to myself, "Man, they must be having a shitty day if they're acting like that. That's too bad." Most of the time, the empathetic explanation is closer to the truth.

Humanity

Whether we like it or not, or admit it or not, we are in deep relationships with people at work. And, like any relationship, we have to invest proper time and attention in it for it to thrive. And for *us* to thrive within it. It takes a long time to develop the emotional foundation of a relationship, and to do that we have to find ways to show our humanity and find humanity in others. We exist in a polarized world right now, and we are just beginning to shake off the strict norms that have governed work for so long. That's a lot for all of us to deal with.

Bring humanity to your workplace. Be vulnerable and honest. Acknowledge when someone else is vulnerable and honest. Ask how people are, and care about their response. Respond to things appropriately but with heart. Be in touch with your heart, even at work.

When people mess up, bring humanity to that too. Forgive what you can, have an open dialogue about what you can't overlook, and always be a part of the change you want to see around you. Also, bring humanity to yourself and accept when something isn't worth pursuing or you have to let something go.

Most humans are just trying to get by, do good work, and be decent to each other. They mess up sometimes. We can find more joy in our daily lives and in our relationships if we keep all of this top of mind. Will you forget and get pissed sometimes? For sure. But if you don't let that consume everything, you will be in a much better place.

You can't make people understand you, but you can make it as easy as possible for them to do so.

Tools for Talking

You can apply these tools to any type of conversation: delivering hard news, speaking up at a meeting, raising a red flag with your boss, breaking up with your girlfriend. Oh, wait. Well, actually, yes, it would work then too. Such flexible advice!

Tools alone won't make you a great communicator; you have to do the work for that. But the tools will help you pause, reflect, and make the best decisions you can at the moment.

T.H.I.N.K.

I can't find the exact origin of this tool and acronym, but it's great, and we should all thank whoever developed it.

Use T.H.I.N.K. by asking yourself these questions before you say something—positive or negative:

T—Is it truthful? Is what you're about to say an objective truth or your opinion or a feeling you have? Truths, opinions, and feelings can be and should be expressed, of course, but how you phrase them will differ. Your feelings are not objective truth; they are your truth.

H—Is it helpful? Generally speaking, we should only be communicating things that are helpful. Now, I know something might not feel helpful in the short run—like negative feedback—but if you believe it is, then a logical and clear explanation of *how* it is helpful can go far during those conversations.

I—Is it inspiring? You might be thinking, "What? I have to be inspiring with my communication?! Can't I just be clear and direct?" Yes, that's a great place to start, but no matter what we're saying, we are trying to have an impact. We are hoping the other person will do something with what we've communicated. All good work is sparked by some inspiration. And when two people meet around a good idea, the results can be brilliant. *If* they are inspired. By working to make your communications inspiring, you are centering potential and possibility and getting the other person on board with whatever you're saying.

I think the best solutions, and the best work, are collaborative. If I can count on you and if you make sense to me, I will trust you. This is also helpful when one of us is the bearer of bad news: if I trust you, those conversations are easier because I know you're on my team and have my back. That all starts with us and how we *choose* to inspire, build up, and connect with our words.

N—Is it necessary? This is a key question. We all have things we *want* to say to people, but, if we're being honest, not all of it *needs* to be said. We need only think of the mansplainers out there contributing pointless opinions to remember that sometimes we should just keep our mouths shut. When we consider how our words are actually contributing, we can get a little more strategic and purposeful with them.

There are two risks to this question, however. First, women are more likely to answer no because we tend to undervalue our ideas. Don't do that, 'K? Thanks. Second, we all might talk ourselves out of speaking up with an unpopular opinion, or one that goes against the majority, by saying to ourselves, "Well, it's not going to make a difference, so it's probably not necessary that I bring it up." These might be the *most* necessary times to speak up. Different opinions are an important element in driving the best outcomes at work because diverse perspectives breed more complete ideas.[42] Challenges to an idea force the team or the person to explain and examine the idea from multiple angles. So that unpopular opinion? Say it. Say it respectfully, but say it.

K—Is it kind? As you will see in the next chapter, I think kindness is an underrated element in life, especially at work. Kindness means we are thinking about the other person and their feelings. A kind approach is considerate. By asking yourself if your contribution is kind, it (hopefully) keeps you from acting on impulsive emotions.

If the answer to any of these questions is no, you'll know you might not be coming from a truly supportive place. Honesty—with yourself and others—is hard. T.H.I.N.K. helps you get real with yourself and keeps your realness with others in the fair and effective zone.

---

42 Alison Reynolds and David Lewis, "Teams Solve Problems Faster When They're More Cognitively Diverse," *Harvard Business Review*, March 30, 2017, https://hbr.org/2017/03/teams-solve-problems-faster-when-theyre-more-cognitively-diverse, and David Rock, Heidi Grant, and Jacqui Grey, "Diverse Teams Feel Less Comfortable — and That's Why They Perform Better," *Harvard Business Review*, September 22, 2016, https://hbr.org/2016/09/diverse-teams-feel-less-comfortable-and-thats-why-they-perform-better.

Boundary Building for the Better

In a world where people are being direct and honest and open at work, we will also need to learn new tools for managing the information. That's where boundaries come in.

I learned about boundaries the hard way: from being young and dumb, occasionally codependent, and an entrepreneur. I also learned about them from my spouse, who, I think I mentioned, is a therapist. What I've come to realize about boundaries is that they are amazing and also one of the last things we think about when it comes to work relationships. If we think of any boundary at work, it's the boundary between work life and life life. We think about personal/professional boundaries, but there are so many other angles at play. There are boundaries between people, emotions, ideas, and opinions.

Bringing a deeper understanding of boundaries to work keeps some of the messiness we embraced in the last chapter from overtaking us when things get hard (which they will). Boundaries allow you to be empathetic without being codependent. Boundaries allow you to see, hear, and acknowledge others without taking on their energy. Boundaries help you set appropriate filters for your emotions. Boundaries help establish how you want to be treated and how you treat others.

Boundaries can be categorized in three ways:

- Physical—personal space and touch considerations
- Mental—thoughts and opinions
- Emotional—feelings

More than these specific types of boundaries, I think it's important to think about how they function out in the world when we're interacting with people. Some boundaries keep your stuff—thoughts, emotions, opinions—in, and some boundaries keep other people's stuff out. In her book *Facing Codependence*, Pia Mellody calls these containing boundaries and protective boundaries. Both are important, and both can be good or bad (as in productive and effective, or unproductive and damaging).

Keeping stuff in is related to emotional intelligence and knowing what of yourself to share with others. When this boundary isn't managed well, you get to the overshare or "TMI" moment. We all know that person at work who shares all their stresses, fears, or complaints about a project and in doing so brings down the whole team's mood and morale. Are you that person? Do you need others around you to know every thought, feeling, and idea you have? If you're silently raising your hand, that's okay! You can work on it. Start by setting some boundaries.

I had one colleague who was quite toxic, but I couldn't put my finger on why. She was a high performer, got along well with her team, and was very smart. Not a typical recipe for disaster, right? But after working at the company for a while, she admitted to her manager that she often approached change or issues at work with frustration and anxiety.

We all have first reactions, and that was generally hers. Once I heard this, I figured out why she felt so toxic. She didn't manage those reactions well—they spilled all over and onto the people around her. So while they *liked* her, her reactions affected others without them entirely knowing how. She didn't know how she was affecting the team, either. While she was self-aware enough to tune in to her own emotions, she hadn't quite connected that those same emotions—unless managed appropriately—would have a cascading effect on those around her. She was in need of containing boundaries.

Keeping other people's stuff out relates to not allowing yourself to absorb what other people are externalizing *or* what you think they are putting out there. For example, when someone says, "That's fine," they might really mean it, and yet you could read into that F word and think, "Oh, it must not be fine. That's the word people always use when they're being passive-aggressive—when they really mean it's not fine." Instead of taking their statement at face value, you take it on yourself and maybe even adjust your own behaviors to adapt to your reaction to their reaction. See how that is so complicated? Maybe even overly complicated? It's because of a lack of boundaries.

I know this scenario pretty well because I am bad at keeping stuff out. If a person is feeling stressed, sad, or overwhelmed, I want to do something immediately to make it better. I *feel* it with them and step into action. If I sense that they aren't fine when they say they are, I want to change course to try to make it fine. Which, in the end, probably just confuses them.

Boundaries require you to be tuned into your physical, mental, and emotional states. When someone lacks the containing boundary, it feels like they are spilling all over. When they lack the protective kind, it feels like they are constantly cleaning up invisible spills. All that at once creates a chaotic and messy space. But when you start paying attention to the flow between you and other people, how you are or are not drawing boundaries, it becomes pretty clear pretty quickly. Fixing boundaries takes a bit more time, but it's worth the effort.

The Four Agreements

Speaking of boundaries! . . . The book I recommend the most to every person, whether at work or not, is *The Four Agreements* by Don Miguel Ruiz. The boundaries and guidelines it sets are so relevant at work when things are often moving quickly, people have a million things on their minds, and stress is eating away at everyone. They are especially salient when thinking about your communication with others—whichever side of the communication you're on. They are:

1. Always do your best.
2. Be impeccable with your word.
3. Don't make assumptions.
4. Don't take things personally.

The two agreements that hit home for me, especially at work, are the last two: don't make assumptions and don't take things personally. Holy crap. How many of our conversations would go more smoothly if we asked a question instead of making an assumption or if we didn't expect that everything was about *us*? How much stress would be avoided if we didn't take on what we *think* someone means? Most people go through their days thinking of themselves, just like you do. You're worried about your budget, car, kids, cat, weekend plans, parents. So is the person communicating with you. They aren't thinking about you at all. But they think you're thinking about them. See how taking things personally creates a constellation of thoughts and feelings that are 100 percent made up?

So take a break from this book and go read *The Four Agreements*. You, your colleagues, and maybe even your friends will thank me.

Cut the Jargon

I'm so sick of jargon, MBA-speak, and acronyms that don't mean anything. All this "business language" is really in service of one goal: making some people feel secure in their place in the hierarchy and others feel insecure about their places. Convoluted terms make straightforward projects sound mystical, and hazy language intimates that certain people know things that no one else does. But the real results are exclusion and information hoarding.

Most work that most of us do, day in and day out, is not that complex. (Except rocket scientists—you do some complex stuff. I thank you. Astronauts thank you.) It behooves no one to exclude people by ensuring that language is opaque or expecting others to reply in the same jargon. Work should not be mystical. That just leaves power in the hands of people who already have it. Work should (and can!) be talked about in accessible language, but too often, language is used to keep people out rather than inviting them in. People use jargon or industryspeak because they are lazy. They don't want to invest time in being thoughtful about what they are saying.

Speaking in clear language shows your real smarts. It shows that you know what you're talking about *and* how to say it in a way that everyone can understand. The smartest people in any room are the ones who can engage with everyone.

It's tough to let go of impulses to show off and prove your superiority. But in reality, it's not necessary to prove how much you know every time you open your mouth. You're not auditioning—you've already got the part, and your chops will be obvious even if you talk like a normal person. What would be a successful outcome for any given meeting or email? Serve *that* goal in the way you speak, not the goal of sounding like you are competing for a summer fellowship.

This doesn't mean that all industry vocabulary should (or can) disappear. I work in the technology industry, and we have to get specific about what we do. We use specialized vocabulary to build connections with clients' actual needs and to communicate what an effective digital partnership is. But describing digital products and services as "best in class," "enterprise quality," or "best practices" means nothing. Ditch the marketing speak and say what you're really doing.

Different people handle these situations differently—and often the approaches are split between men and women. I've watched men fake mastery while women refuse to commit to any amount of expertise in a space where they're mildly confused. Men routinely exhibit confidence far beyond their abilities, while women hold back for a litany of internalized social reasons like worrying about appearing too smart, not wanting to take up too much space, not feeling like their ideas are welcome, and many more. Women are busy being overly careful, and men rarely have filters.

The best tack is somewhere in the middle. Ditch enough fear to speak up when and how you need to, and have enough emotional intelligence to know when to step up and when to listen. Here are a few tips for getting to that point:

- Find a mentor or a sponsor: someone inside your organization with whom you can be perfectly candid. Practice breaking ideas down into nonjargon concepts and use them when you're confused about jargon someone else uses.

- Be confident enough to say, "I don't know, but I'm going to find out." Then find out.

- Develop the habit of researching content you don't understand. Read up and take notes. Knowing the business is the best way to get ahead and be seen.

Competence breeds confidence.

Talking—and Hearing—Better

We just went through *a lot* of information. I know, and I can almost hear you saying, "If only there were a template for thoughtfully saying whatever thing I need to communicate!" Lucky for you, there is! Kind of. A starting point, at least, and a few strategies to help you down the thoughtful path.

Tough Messages

Delivering Better

When you have something hard to say, it can be overwhelming. Yet hard things need to be said—often—and they can help move relationships, partnerships, and projects forward in healthy ways when done well. I have spent a lot of time in my career trying to find decent, human, and effective ways of sharing crappy news because I believe you can get much further with people if you're forward and direct. It builds trust, camaraderie, and understanding.

If you're the one delivering a tough message to a colleague or client, here are some things to try.

Identify *why* you are telling them the thing. Not what the thing is, or what you hope they will do in response to the thing, but why it is important that you tell them the thing.

Finish the sentence: "My goal is that you hear ____." The blank could be "the operations team's perspective," or "why Sonya is confused." And then you stop. It's tempting to bleed right into "and I hope you do this in response," but at this point in the conversation, any direction of someone's actions is overstepping. Don't control, just clarify.

I've had moments where I realized, when I'm most honest with myself, that my goal in communicating was not very helpful. Perhaps I kind of wanted to make the other person feel bad in some way (probably in a defensive move), or I was scared and lashing out (again, probably defensively). Or maybe I wanted to feel "right," have them feel responsible for a failure, feel inferior to me, whatever. Those are never my best moments, but I have them. You have them. We all have them.

I'm not here to condemn you if you've done that too. But I am here to say that when you do catch that instinct in yourself, don't have that conversation. Not yet, not right then. If the issue is meaningful, and not a knee-jerk emotional reaction, then take the time to identify a less personal, more purposeful reason for why you need to say something. Conversations are shaped by each party's goal, so a well-intentioned goal produces healthier communication.

Sharing your "why" with someone else establishes candor in the relationship. It sets boundaries for the conversation, creating both safety and focus. It clarifies intent. And it removes from the other person the burden of having to read between the lines, interpret what you're thinking, or guess at further context. There's nothing bad about clearly stating your goal (though directness can be scary, but we've already talked about that).

Don't be afraid to run your lines before a conversation: thoughtful communication takes practice, and no instance is too small to be worth nailing. Rehearse the "why," and practice ending your statement once you've said what you need to. If you catch yourself rambling, stop. Give the other person time and space to think.

Ask for their help. People are programmed to want to show up when asked to help, and whether or not you *actually* feel like you need help, framing your position and message in a way that asks them to participate gives them agency. Asking for help also makes tough messages feel less isolating: it casts you as one of the key players, and it casts you and the recipient as a *team*, which feels better for everyone than an isolated island. A one-sided conversation is a soliloquy at best, an attack at worst.

Before I deliver a hard message, I might say, "This is going to be hard for me to say; I need your help in being patient while we process it all." Or if I'm about to ask more of them, I might say, "The project is really struggling, and I need your help in getting it back on track." I tried this approach earlier in my career because I really wanted help. My request always was and is genuine. I do want help. I want whoever I'm addressing to be *with* me on getting to the other side of the conversation productively and together. I do want them to be invested in what I'm saying and what we need to do to get beyond that moment.

Asking for help might make you feel weak at first, especially if you're talking to a client or a higher-up at work. But, first, everyone needs help, and it's silly that we all beat around that bush. Second, the magic is in what you ask them to help with. If you lead with "I can't handle this situation, I need help," your expertise or contribution might be questioned. Now reposition it as "I thought this was going to go differently; can you help me rethink my strategy?" How much better will that question land?

Provide a thoughtful rationale. This goes back to the value of context. The other person's thoughts, mindset, and emotions will be different than yours in that moment when the conversation starts. The rationale will not only provide the context that will help explain your message but also give them time to process. Going into it, let them know you are going to provide the context, almost like a roadmap.

If, as in the example above, "My goal is that you hear the operation team's perspective," the next part of your message might go something like, "We have three points that we've all put a lot of thought into, and we'd like to share them." Then, of course, you share the points. By the time you're done sharing your points, you both may very well be on the same page emotionally.

The difficult message will be in there among the goal, the request for help, and the rationale. It won't get lost, but hopefully it will get contextualized and wrapped with a little humanity.

Receiving Better

Of course, sometimes you're on the other end of the conversation: receiving tough messages. I'm not even talking strictly about receiving negative feedback—there's a whole feedback section for that below. I'm talking about how you take in and respond to things you don't want to hear. Things like, "We're over budget on your project," or, "I need you to dress more appropriately for work," or, "The department is going through some changes and you will be impacted." Really different messages, but all hard to hear.

One of the best gifts we can give another person is to be a good and productive listener. We have all been on the delivery end of a tough message and know how hard it can be. Being gracious, open, and receptive to hearing what someone has to say, even when it's hard—or maybe especially when it's hard—can make all the difference in working well with others and finding your power in the tough moments.

Actively participating as a listener can also make it easier *for you* to hear the message. Here are some tips for being a good recipient of tough messages.

Focus on the intention. Most people we engage with at work don't have crappy intentions. It certainly happens *sometimes,* but aside from the few jerks we all have to deal with, most people are trying to get their work done well and with as few complications as possible. Going into conversations assuming good intent is not only more helpful, it is often also correct. You might have to imagine their intention if they haven't done a great job of setting it up, but that process can help reorient your immediate reaction to something helpful.

Pay attention to more than the center of the bull's-eye. The center of the target is the news. It's the thing that you don't want to hear. Because of that, it's easy to dwell on it. Your emotions are triggered, and then you want to perseverate. Avoid that, at least for the moment. It's not going to be helpful, and besides, our brains will probably dwell on that well after the conversation. (On the way home in the car! When we're trying to fall asleep! There's plenty of time!) So give yourself a little gift and set aside that initial freakout while you think about the context and rationale. Ask whatever questions you have to in order to start seeing the layers of whys and hows around the tough center.

Remember the shared goal. Bad news, changes, and new information arrive at work all the time. You can let them derail your attention and energy, or you can redirect that attention and energy to adapting to the news and folding it into your perspective. Thinking about the shared goal will help you with that. When I hear news I don't want to get, I always have to consciously take a few metaphorical steps back and think about my shared goal with the person or group I'm hearing from. Ask yourself, "What are we trying to do, and how can I use this new information to still get there?"

If the person delivering the message isn't making the goal or common interest clear, ask them to discuss that. Getting focused on a shared outcome can be powerful and motivating for both of you. If it feels like they are making a one-sided argument (or a selfish one), ask them to reframe so you can see the bigger picture. You have a responsibility to understand what they're saying, and that means productively engaging until you do.

Share concern in thoughtful ways. If you are having a difficult time receiving the message or making sense of it, say that. Share what is on your mind as clearly as possible. You can be mad, upset, hurt, or nervous about whatever you're hearing, but lashing out or shutting down won't move the needle on the issue or the conversation. And boy, do I know that's hard. Our flight-or-fight responses kick in, and we want to do anything other than be cooperative. If you need time to get your thoughts together, say that too. Acknowledge what you heard and ask if you can take a little time to respond. Here are a few scripts to keep on hand:

- I hear your perspective. Can I take some time to gather my thoughts and reach back out to you tomorrow?

- I am nervous about what this means; my biggest concern is _____. Can we discuss that more in depth?

- I am hurt by what you're saying, but I can appreciate your point.

Sharing Your Ideas

Getting good at sharing your ideas is one of the most useful things you can do to feel more empowered at work. On the surface, this might sound easy. Ideas are fun! (Definitely more fun than bad news.) But if you've ever found yourself in your boss's office or in a client meeting, trying to convince them of something and feeling like you're speaking a foreign language, you will remember how hard it is and keep reading. If you've never felt like that, hooray! It's not fun. Keep reading to avoid that.

Show how it adds value. Work is business, which means outcomes matter. No company, boss, or colleague is going to be all-in on an idea that doesn't advance the organization's mission, vision, or bottom line. Period. You can want something all day long, but if it doesn't make business sense, then it should be set aside. If it does, ask yourself these questions when thinking about presenting it to your team.

- What is the intended outcome?

- What problem is it fixing?

- What research or evidence do you have to support your idea?

- What is the most likely counterargument? Now, disprove that.

Share credit where it's due, and keep yourself open to collaboration. No idea is done and fully baked right out of the gate. Innovation and new ideas come from working with other people who bring new perspectives and divergent ideas to the table. By sharing credit, you're acknowledging the indirect path our ideas take. None of us does anything alone, and saying that you do doesn't make you look smarter—it makes you look like a terrible team player.

If a new perspective comes in after you think your idea is "done," don't shut it down. Nothing is really done anymore. All businesses are looking for continuous improvement and iterations that keep them ahead of the curve. Your one idea won't be stagnant for long, so go into it with that mindset. Getting buy-in and input helps build your case. When people are participating, you will hear more honest reactions and start to build a team around the idea, and they will feel more invested.

Ask for feedback. Keep yourself explicitly and honestly open to what people think. And listen. Unless you ask, you might not get authentic feedback. If they have negative feedback, they might be scared to bring it up. If they have challenging questions, they might not know if you want to hear them. All feedback is data for you to make your idea—and how you present it—stronger.

If your ideas aren't heard, it's no one's fault but your own. People shouldn't have to ask you what you think. And people can't know how good your idea is if you don't convince them. Speak up, and keep trying if it doesn't work the first time. Listen to what they say and watch how they react. Use that next time around to make a stronger case and more persuasive presentation. Good ideas come from everywhere—high up in the CEO's office and on the pavement in the sales meeting. But *we* have to find the route to sharing our ideas: no one owes us that.

Talking Up

Talking up is the cousin of sharing your ideas, but it's more about raising a flag, asking for change, or calling out an error. These are messages we have to think about very carefully at work. Delivering a message up the food chain is one of the hardest things in a workplace—most of the time, people just write it off as impossible. But this type of communication is necessary and key to finding your voice and power.

As an employee, you get your boss's perspective on your work, but bosses are often shielded from your perspective on their work or the work going on around the office. Many leaders tout their open-door policies without creating them in real life. And many employees are apprehensive about speaking honestly, though they might wish to.

Anytime you create pushback up the food chain, you risk repercussions and retaliation, but you can take two steps to significantly reduce those risks.

Gain their trust. Gaining trust is the same in any relationship: it requires time. Invest weeks and months into showing up, keeping your promises, and setting your ego aside. Consider why your leader might be making the decisions they do, and get creative in your willingness to see their point of view.

Rolling into their office with guns blazing and pointing out all the things that could be better won't make you any friends. Not everything they do might be *right,* but they have likely been doing it for longer than you, so you can assume they do know something. Figure out what things look like from their position.

Prove your value. People believe and want to hear from individuals who have demonstrated they know their stuff. You don't have to know everything to say anything, but if you haven't made a contribution to the work, your criticism of it might not go over well.

Gaining trust and proving your value establishes a relationship that becomes vital to your leader's career, which puts you in a position to be honest about the changes you'd like to see. Prove that you are acting in the best interests of them and the organization, rather than yourself, your ego, or your resume.

And, just like I've said before, consider why you want to provide feedback to your boss. If you just want to see them fail, you're setting *yourself* up for failure. It doesn't matter how pretty your words are; people are excellent at reading negative intentions. No one wants to feel attacked, especially in a hierarchy.

The F Word

Speaking of feeling attacked: buckle up folks, we're finally talking feedback! Feedback is the hardest tough message of all. I wanted to bookend this section with this topic because I know how hard it can be to receive and deliver feedback, and I know how valuable both can be to growing at work and developing better relationships. Many of us cower at the thought of these conversations, and in that cowering, we slowly lose credibility, confidence, and power. Feedback will seldom be easy or bring you joy, but it can be effective and productive, which can feel really damn good at work.

Before we dig in, I want to share something I learned from my spouse that helps me immeasurably when receiving and giving feedback. It's the related concepts of wounded child, adaptive child, and functional adult. Pia Mellody outlined these concepts in *Facing Codependence*. Stick with me here, because while they were originally conceived in the context of codependence, I see elements of them in how individuals act at work. They are useful models for thinking about our emotional selves and at what stage of the continuum we might fall at particular moments. Let's dig in a bit more.

The wounded child is the part of us that holds and feels the pain from our past. Even if we had mostly delightful childhoods, we all faced something difficult and it's still with us.

Our inner child wants what it wants and tends to react emotionally, not cognitively. Forever infant- to toddler-aged, this child feels inferior to others and reacts to things with literal or metaphorical tantrums, outbursts, or impulsive behaviors. Our inner children are needy and want validation and attention, and negative observations feel like the exact opposite. I've heard a colleague explain that criticism makes him feel like his "best work isn't seen." That's an inner-child response.

The adaptive child is the slightly more grown-up version of our young, wounded soul. This child has adapted to the environment and learned how to survive. This version of our inner child knows how to cope and react, but does so in adolescent-like ways. Our adaptive child feels superior to others, shuts down during hard conversations (we've all seen this in actual adolescents), and has out-of-scale protective boundaries that keep people and information at arm's length (but *never* their accountability).

The functional adult is the mature version of yourself. Functional adults (as is suggested by the name) react, interact, and engage more appropriately. They feel equal to others; they do not need to tear down others to feel better because they have boundaries and respect other people's boundaries. They are aware of their own wounds and insecurities from early childhood, their inner-child and adaptive-child urges, and how to manage all that. Functional adults can give and receive hard messages without resorting to childish responses.

The truth is, critical feedback can always feel like trauma. It can always trigger some leftover memory or reaction that was buried deep after a negative situation in the past. Maybe your first boss was mean and said terrible things in front of your coworkers. Maybe you had a teacher in elementary school that embarrassed you—I had a few of those. One, who was also my basketball coach, was mean to me because I wasn't very good at the game. Instead of helping or, well, *coaching* me, she made fun of me in front of my teammates. Guess how I feel about basketball and gyms? Go back even earlier than school and we'll find how our parents shared their opinions of us with us. All of us experienced something that made us feel bad when we were children, and it's still part of us—we can call it our wounded child, like Mellody does, or just our inner child. Either way, we all have them, and they do not behave like adults. They are encoded in our mental and muscle memory, and we have to work really hard to react in other ways.

I often think of these models when I'm in a feedback conversation. It is easy to regress, even though we all wish we were functional adults every hour of the day. I say things and am immediately aware that my wounded child is coming out. Now that I know that, it's easier to deal with. Because I can name it, I can also say, "Dang, that was my snappy adaptive child attacking you. I'm sorry. Let's try that again, and I will try to do better." (Okay, I don't actually say that. But you get the idea.) It's about owning behaviors I want to change.

Meghan, my best friend, former coauthor, and colleague, once told me I have a bad habit of finishing other people's sentences. I felt so dumb when she said it, and I immediately got very defensive—well, my adaptive child got defensive. But she was right, and damn it, I still do it. I have little patience! (Not an excuse, I know.) But I now have an awareness of it because she cared enough to tell me. And I definitely work my listening muscle more often and more intentionally because of that feedback. But, I mean—imagine hearing that? Not easy.

Taking Feedback

I always hear about people struggling to connect to their inner child in a good way (the unadulterated joy! the unfettered trust!), but the one time I see *everyone* connect to their inner child is when they're receiving critical feedback. I do it too. My inner and adaptive children are right there, ready to react before my thoughtful functional adult realizes what's up.

A recent experience reminded me of how fragile I am, even after all these years of giving and hearing feedback. My company had just received a review on an employment website, and the reviewer wrote some pretty specific and pointed things about my company and me personally. It hurt my feelings a lot—I was sad that someone I worked with thought those things about me and the place I put so much of myself and energy into. Then I got very defensive, denying that anything about the comment was true at all. Then I got angry at the person for never giving me the opportunity to hear their perspective from them and have a dialogue about it (it's an anonymous website). And then, after a while, I was finally able to step back and look at the review and the situation more objectively. That is, until I started talking about it with others at work, and my initial emotions kept flooding back. My mind said, "I'm being honest and open," but my words and energy said, "I want to kick that person's butt."

In the end, I realized the reviewer was trying to be hurtful and mean, not productive and constructive. I can't do anything about that, and it wasn't useful for me to take that on. I used it as an example with my colleagues of what *not* to do if you actually want to make things better at work or for yourself at work. Throwing a complaint grenade over an anonymous wall doesn't make anything better—most of all not you because you're robbing yourself of an opportunity to make helpful suggestions, improve your communication skills, and build stronger bonds at work by building a better workplace. If you don't want to do any of that, then quit (which I'm pretty sure they did).

The whole experience was a big reminder of the advice I'm sharing here. I had to not take it personally, even though it mentioned me specifically (very hard to do), and I had to make my peace with it and find a way to learn from the feedback (also very hard to do). This unfolded and refolded over the course of a few months. It was a big challenge for me to let go of what I needed to about it all and take what was useful. It took me time to figure all that out. I wish it was quick and easy for me—and all of us—but it's not. Being an adult can be hard.

Here are a few of the things I try to (and, as you see, sometimes fail to) keep in mind when I'm getting feedback from people.

Don't take it personally. After reading *The Four Agreements* ten-plus years ago, I began coaching myself to not take negative feedback personally . . . and yet, my first reaction is always defensiveness. It's a tough habit to break. We want to seek flaws in the other person, ulterior motives—any explanation that makes it not our fault.

There is no magic way to not take things personally. I wish there were. But sometimes even saying that to yourself (don't take it personally, don't take it personally) can defuse your immediate emotional response. Even saying it out loud can help.

Ask for what you need in the moment. If you need a moment to process, take it. Saying, "Thank you for saying that. I would like to think about it before I react so I can be intentional with how we proceed" is a hell of a lot better than reacting from a place of defensiveness ("What?! How dare you!?") or fear ("Oh shit, am I going to lose my job?!") If you take time, you can bypass your lizard-brain reaction, talk it out with a trusted colleague or friend, and come back to the conversation with more perspective.

An aspect of having good boundaries is being self-aware enough to know how to react appropriately. If you're not in the headspace to be the person you want to be in the moment, you will do your future and your colleague a favor by acknowledging that. But remember, it's on you to assess, bring it up, and suggest a solution. As in our romantic relationships, the other person is not a mind reader.

Find the positive in it. The toughest lesson anyone learns in a workplace is that negative observations are opportunities for evolution and betterment. Just one individual accepting tough feedback thoughtfully helps to build healthier and more effective communication patterns in an organization. There are plenty of memes on Instagram to remind us that "discomfort means we're growing" or "the hardest rains create the brightest rainbows." While these might make you gag, the core message can be true if you make it so: learn from all the hard stuff. Find something to take away and grow from.

We all have blind spots, and ignoring yours is resigning yourself to a stagnant career (and life). If you're not interested in growth, I'm frankly shocked you've made it this far in the book. Put the book down! Go back to the same old same old!

For the more calculating readers, consider that letting yourself be humbled in front of someone can be powerful. Leverage doesn't need to be rooted in hierarchical authority; leverage can be rooted in the respect you gain from someone when you listen to them.

Clarify instead of arguing. Our adaptive child wants to argue and prove the other person wrong (because you're better than them! Duh!), but that won't feel good or get you very far. Feedback can raise a lot of questions within us—about our worth and our value, but also about our performance and contributions. You might need some of those questions answered to process and grow. Get the clarity you can.

If you don't understand where the feedback is coming from, ask for more information. Say, "I hear you, but I am having a hard time getting on the same page. Can you explain it again to help me see it from your perspective?" or "My perception of the presentation was different, can we walk through specifics?"

Giving Feedback

Giving critical feedback is difficult for the same reason it's hard to hear it: it feels personal. People get so emotionally attached to work that it's hard to separate the person from the product. But an environment without discussion of flaws is one without evolution. So it's critical that we get critical—constructively.

When giving feedback, there is one thing you absolutely must do no matter what: you have to really care. You have to care about the other person, the outcome of the conversation, the common interest you both have in the work, and the quality of the environment you're in. If you don't care about that, don't give feedback. Seriously. If you don't care about the person, nothing you say will land right and you will both be worse for it. If you don't give enough of a shit about the people you manage to dig up actual interest in their work, quit being a manager. Everything is better when you care.

The basics: Be respectful. Don't be condescending. Treat the person's ideas like they matter.

As in all communication, reflect on *why* you want to say what you want to say. Over the years, I have come to realize that lots of feedback is actually just venting about another person. Do yourself a favor and share those grievances with your best friend first. Polish your feedback until it is productive, and then have the conversation.

And now, finer points.

Identify your desired outcome. Just like tough messages, feedback goes over much better when you present the outcome you're hoping for from the conversation. We all know what we hope for won't necessarily happen, but being crystal clear about where you hope you can get with the conversation will remove some of the personal crap that is bound to come up both in you and the other person.

Ask for their perspective first. Engage them in the issue, and demonstrate that their point of view has value. Ask, "What were you hoping would be different in that meeting?" or "Can you explain why you made this decision?" Constructive criticism shouldn't be a one-way street. Giving the other person the floor eliminates the feeling of being trapped, tricked, or disrespected.

Be thoughtful, not careful. It is damn scary to speak directly about work at work because, for most of us, work is deeply personal. Our self-worth and self-value are bound up in our professions and our success at our jobs. Next time you deliver a message that is anything less than celebratory—not necessarily even flat-out negative—consider your communication on a spectrum from careful to thoughtful. Careful centers you and your discomfort. It is more about how *you* feel than it is about the message itself or the other person. When we're being careful we are avoidant, indirect, unclear, and passive-aggressive. We editorialize and apologize, soften and couch. When we do all this, we aren't being honest. Guess what, folks: that's all bad news. Without any communication, issues fester. Without direct communication, issues get blurred or neutered.

Thoughtful communication centers the other person. A thoughtfully delivered message is considerate of their feelings without shrinking or obscuring the message. When we empathize with and humanize the other person, when we take accountability for our own discomfort and

move through it, and when we know we're trying to make a positive impact by saying what we're about to say, we can be thoughtful.

When we're too careful, we dilute the message . . . and sometimes don't communicate it at all. When we're thoughtful, we do our best to communicate with everyone's best interests in mind.

You're smart, so you're probably seeing some patterns within all this advice: keep your cool, ask questions, make it about the work and not yourself, and don't be afraid to pause and come back to something.

Work Like a Boss Takeaways

1. It's okay if communication is hard for you, but you absolutely have to work on it to be effective at work and find your personal power.
2. Bring context, intention, empathy, and humanity to every conversation, interaction, and engagement with people.
3. Use tools to get better. Practice and ask for feedback. Know that everyone else is trying too.

Chapter Seven

BE F*ING KIND

We're almost at the end, and you've gotten to what will sound like the easiest path to increased fulfillment at work: be effing kind. Phew, that sounds doable! But I think we all know that some of the simplest things are, at the same time, also the hardest things. That is kindness in a nutshell.

Remember when I said that I wouldn't tell you anything you didn't already know? Well, kindness is definitely that. It's the Golden Rule that we all learned in kindergarten and then sidelined because, for a lot of people, it doesn't come naturally. Here's the thing: everything that I'm about to say will feel really obvious, but it's not. At least, it's not obvious in the way we generally operate at work.

When I first moved to the Twin Cities from Michigan, a friend hooked me up with a job at a music and software distribution company. I received boxes of returned inventory, opened the boxes, peeled the original price tags off the CDs and DVDs, and then put them into a different box. Open, peel, place. All. Day. Long. Oh, and I couldn't ruin the plastic wrapping around the merchandise. I was in a giant warehouse

with no windows, and I sat at an uncomfortable desk. I was grateful for the job at a time when I needed it, but I was also hoping that it would lead to additional opportunities at the company. I worked most closely with two women who processed the merchandise in our inventory system. They had been there far longer than me and knew each other pretty well. And they both were terrible to me. When I asked questions, they would roll their eyes. They treated me like I was the dumbest person on Earth, and it was demoralizing. So not only was I bored, but I also had the luck to be assigned to a team of two of the meanest human beings.

I needed this job; I needed *a* job. I was living in a rattrap of an apartment, I had sold my car in Michigan to move to the city, and here I was, completely miserable. I can take crappy work, but being treated like crap by colleagues made my life unbearable. They could have been kind, and they were not. They chose something else. They chose to create a culture of exclusion.

I couldn't function in that environment, so I left. In retrospect, that was a privilege that as a white, educated young woman I believed I could (barely) afford, but it was also an act of self-preservation. And this wasn't the only time I quit a job when the people around me made me feel less-than. If I had let those people make *me* into what they believed I should be, I would never have gotten anywhere. I hope they learned somewhere along the way to be kinder to colleagues. How you treat people, how you welcome and respect people, and how you create a sense of belonging create opportunities for you and them.

Looking back, this early experience indelibly influenced how I behave at work. They were rude, and it felt bad. They were dismissive, and I felt excluded. They were unkind, and that prevented me from doing a good job.

Kindness is strange. It's basic, human behavior that we often have to work hard to cultivate. We have to be very intentional if we want to bring kindness to our jobs and to our colleagues. As we get older, more jaded, and more complacent, kindness gets less and less habitual for us. We all know this in our bones, even if we don't want to admit it. I read an article about the ways complaining rewires our brains. It said, "Your brain loves efficiency and doesn't like to work any harder than it has to. When you repeat a behavior, such as complaining, your neurons branch out to each other to ease the flow of information."[43] When I read this, I felt validated: negativity feels easier because it is. On the flip side, if we start to rewire our brains with kindness, perhaps that would be easier. Perhaps we can build new neuron branches that default to something more gracious and inclusive, and, in turn, we can feel better about work and ourselves.

43 Travis Bradberry, "How Complaining Rewires Your Brain for Negativity," *Entrepreneur*, September 9, 2016, https://www.entrepreneur.com/article/281734.

To see the bright side, we have to choose it.

The Case for Kindness

If you're thinking, "I don't want to be kind to Mike, that guy bugs the hell out of me," or, "Everyone at my office is so crappy, I don't think being kind will do anything," I hear you! But there's something in it for you. (This whole book *is* about finding *your* power and increased fulfillment at work).

Being kind feels good to you and makes other people feel good. Being kind makes others respond with kindness. Kindness is the shortest route to building connections with other people. And that advances the joy factor. A longitudinal study at Harvard showed that close relationships, more than money or fame, are what keep people happy throughout their lives.[44] You don't have to wait to get a promotion, beat that other guy for the new C-suite role, or buy a nicer car or . . . anything. You can be happier by simply spreading a little good energy and developing strong supporting relationships at work.

---

44 Liz Mineo, "Good Genes are Nice, but Joy Is Better," *Harvard Gazette*, April 11, 2017, https://news.harvard.edu/gazette/story/2017/04/over-nearly-80-years-harvard-study-has-been-showing-how-to-live-a-healthy-and-happy-life/.

Emotions Spread Quickly

Your energy is contagious, so you *can* have an impact on Mike and all those other people who kind of suck. In a recent article in *Forbes*, Dr. Pragya Agarwal cites a study that put a scientific lens on acts of kindness and found that "kindness really does create a positive ripple that affects the whole workplace culture."[45] Like negativity, positive energy has a ripple effect. What you do actually changes the feelings around you. We've all worked with Sally Sunshines or Donnie Downers and witnessed this science in action. Sally says something positive and makes pleasant conversation. You feel pretty good when you're done chatting. Donnie walks up and immediately starts down a negative path, complaining about the last meeting, the weather, or anything else in view. When you're done chatting with him, you feel blah. He just sucked a little life out of you.

I always say, "Know the energy you're bringing into a room." Contagion is why. I have walked into rooms and killed or elevated moods based on facial expressions. I have rained on parades unknowingly, and have unintentionally cut through awkward silences with a joke. That's how I know this works. Because I've inadvertently affected people, I now try to be

---

45 Pragya Agarwal, "Making Kindness a Priority in the Workplace," *Forbes*, August 26, 2019, https://www.forbes.com/sites/pragyaagarwaleurope/2019/08/26/making-kindness-a-priority-in-the-workplace/#10fae06b38f4.

attentive to the expression on my face and the tone of my voice as I talk to others. They are picking up on it. That's a lot of responsibility, I know, but it's also a lot of power. Our energy is the one thing we can control, and we can use to influence other people.

The L Word at Work

"Whether organizations—and their employees—flounder or flourish largely depends on the quality of the social relationships they possess."[46] Not only is this compelling, but it also goes against so much of what "professionalism" and business have pronounced for decades. Hard skills! Competition! Hustle! Burn the midnight oil! I've gone over how much I disagree with all that already, but this quote gets at something I want to dwell on: the *quality* of relationships at work.

Quality speaks to more than getting along. It speaks to actually engaging and connecting. This made intuitive sense to me after having and witnessing both crappy and quality work relationships, but the work of Dr. Sigal Barsade crystalized (and validated) my intuition. Barsade is an organizational development researcher who has done a ton of work around emotional intelligence and companionate love at work. Her

---

46 Elaine Houston, "The Importance of Positive Relationships in the Workplace," PositivePsychology.com, February 11, 2020, https://positivepsychology.com/positive-relationships-workplace/.

work blew my mind when I first discovered it because it was so well researched and the findings were so human.

Companionate love at work is pretty simple to explain. It's caring. It's shown "when colleagues who are together day in and day out, ask and care about each other's work and even non-work issues," Barsade says. "They are careful of each other's feelings. They show compassion when things don't go well. And they also show affection and caring—and that can be about bringing somebody a cup of coffee when you go get your own, or just listening when a co-worker needs to talk."[47]

She explains that in the history of work, we focus on cognitive culture—and, I would add, cognitive intelligence. We have devalued emotional culture, but it is just as important. She says, "What we're talking about is shared emotions. Our field tends to focus on shared cognitions of people at work, yet an understanding of shared emotions of people at work can also have important outcomes for organizations." In the original study, she found that overall employee engagement increased when the emotional culture was positive. Emotional exhaustion, absenteeism, and burnout decreased. She also discovered "that a culture of

---

47 Wharton School, "Why Fostering a Culture of 'Companionate Love' in the Workplace Matters," Knowledge@Wharton, April 2. 2014, https://knowledge.wharton.upenn.edu/article/fostering-culture-compassion-workplace-matters/.

companionate love led to higher levels of employee engagement with their work via greater teamwork and employee satisfaction."[48]

After reviewing the findings, Barsade also concluded, "It may well be that even if you don't start out feeling the culture of love—even if you're just enacting it—it can lead to these positive outcomes. In addition, there is the possibility that as you enact companionate love, you will begin to feel it over time." Contagion! And perhaps the most beneficial use of faking it 'til you make it. The original study was conducted in a medical care context, but the findings from their subsequent studies in other industries correlated.

It's best if companies lead the way with this approach to employee compassion, but it doesn't have to be happening throughout the organization to feel it. Barsade ends an article about her work, "Most importantly . . . it is the small moments between coworkers—a warm smile, a kind note, a sympathetic ear—day after day, month after month, that help create and maintain a strong culture of companionate love and the

---

48 Sigal G. Barsade and Olivia Amanda O'Neill, "What's Love Got to Do with It? A Longitudinal Study of the Culture of Companionate Love and Employee and Client Outcomes in a Long-term Care Setting," *Administrative Science Quarterly* 59, no. 4 (2014): 551–98, https://www.semanticscholar.org/paper/What%E2%80%99s-Love-Got-to-Do-with-It-A-Longitudinal-Study-Barsade-O'Neill/db249d2782a3161010073edf3d8bfa4577c1bb3e.

employee satisfaction, productivity, and client satisfaction that comes with it."[49]

We aren't taught how to create companionate love. Men aren't because it requires emotional intelligence, which is seen as emasculating and weak. Women aren't because we are taught to compete against each other for the position of "woman unlike other women" in a world largely run by men. So we're left to think we should value only rational intellect, even though we benefit greatly from emotional sensitivity.

The easiest thing you can do to strengthen companionate love is act kindly. I'm not talking about leaving candy on someone's desk or complimenting a sweater. I'm talking about genuine, human kindness. The kind of engagement that requires attention, commitment, and awareness. Companionate love isn't superficial. It's real. It's finding connections and bonds with the people we spend most of our conscious lives with.

Work Relationships Are Just That: Relationships

Relationships at work are like any relationship: they require effort. Think back to a time when you fell in romantic love. At first, you're so excited! You try hard and are on your best behavior. Then you move in together,

49 Sigal Barsade and Olivia A. O'Neill, "Employees Who Feel Love Perform Better," *Harvard Business Review*, January 13, 2014, https://hbr.org/2014/01/employees-who-feel-love-perform-better.

and things get a little harder. You see them for who they really are, and you see *you* for who you are in that relationship. Then things normalize and you start to take things for granted. It's a little harder to be generous and giving and a little easier to see the things that annoy you. When you find someone with whom it works out, you can see the best of them and accept the worst of them. That's how we describe (and hopefully how we *feel*) unconditional love.

While we have all probably talked about that journey or something like it in our personal lives, we never talk about it with work. We seem to reserve all good, fruitful emotional investments for our personal lives and think it's absurd to apply them at our jobs. It's the old-fashioned personal/professional divide working its way through our DNA.

Work and work relationships seem to be entirely conditional. Coworker Beverly does one thing wrong, and we don't like her. Sanjay gave you a look in that marketing meeting, so you never want to have lunch with him. We aren't good at unconditional love, and yet it would serve us well at work. *Not* doing it hasn't gotten us very far, has it?

My partner and I have been together for twenty-six years. In that time, I have seen the best, the worst, and everything in between. I could focus on how her dirty socks never seem to make it into the hamper, or I could focus on the wonderful dinners she cooks for me and our son.

Guess which focus makes our relationship better, and which one makes both of us *feel* better? Hopefully, you guessed the latter.

I wrote a blog a few years back titled, "To See the Bright Side, You Have to Choose It." The bright side, like kindness and positivity and power and joy, is something we have to consciously choose for our day, week, and life. All the little things that are going well, the people with whom we work seamlessly, the day that goes by without a hitch—these moments won't scream at us and tell us to pay attention. And, as we've covered, our brains aren't going to do that either. So, we have to do it ourselves.

What if we saw people at work for who they are and accepted it? Even if it's annoying? We probably (cough, definitely, cough) make little annoyances worse by dwelling rather than looking beyond them to the whole person. Of course the crappy thing is the only thing we will see if that's all we *allow* ourselves to see.

You can't be kind to others if you're not kind to yourself.

The Path to Kindness

If kindness is contagious and builds genuine bonds with people around us, and if bonds are good for us and work, it's clear that we'd better get on the kindness train. I think that's harder for us than we anticipate. Not because we're evil, but because we are selfish and self-centered. We spend most of our time at work thinking about us: how our day is going, our feelings or worries about what's coming up, our to-dos, our insecurities, our . . . everything. Most of those thoughts probably aren't very positive—or kind. They likely involve stress, judgment, worry, and anxiety. I'm painting quite a picture of people at work, eh? I'm sure there is something in there you can see in yourself—or maybe in others around you.

Kindness starts with you. Not just the accountability we've talked about—which is still true—but also being kind *to yourself.* Like many behaviors, kindness is very hard to do genuinely for others if you aren't also extending it to yourself. Technically, you probably *can* do it, but you'll get much further and be much better at it if your self-kindness skills are honed and your kindness reservoir is mostly full.

Self-kindness has many facets. We have to apply the generosity, thoughtfulness, and compassion that define kindness to how we talk to ourselves and how we care for ourselves. That means more than just accepting what we're feeling or going through; it also involves coping and caring for ourselves in ways that move us in a positive direction. While improving our always-present negative self-talk is a good step, an even kinder step is actively supporting ourselves through the tough times.[50]

- It's not judging yourself so harshly while also recognizing your very human limitations. It's engaging in positive, affirming self-talk that builds you up while also building tolerance and self-acceptance to avoid depending on self-talk altogether.

- It's being thankful for what you can and do accomplish and taking the time to appreciate it instead of dwelling on what you didn't get done.

- It's using your break at work to do something productive and positive instead of something that perpetuates your stress, like crappy watercooler griping. Breaks should be actual breaks. Go for a walk, clear your head, be quiet, breathe air. Don't pollute your mind and body during that time.

---

50 A useful article about self-kindness is Beverly Engel's "Using the Practice of Self-Kindness to Cope with Stress," *Psychology Today*, Jun 19, 2018, https://www.psychologytoday.com/us/blog/the-compassion-chronicles/201806/using-the-practice-self-kindness-cope-stress.

When we look more closely at how we can be kind to ourselves, self-care becomes a primary focus. Asking how *you* can actively care for you is more difficult than it sounds. Most of us do not pay attention to what truly fulfills us, nor do we take the time to do those things once we've identified them. Self-care is the antidote to basically all the crappy feelings we have and crappy mindsets we have. Busyness and burnout eat away at our creativity and our energy, and the only way to rebuild those is through self-care.

I was at a conference recently with the founder and CEO of Evereve, a clothing store that began here in the Twin Cities area and now has locations across the country. In her talk, she shared that she didn't know anything about retail when she started her company. As she told the story of her path to success and how she manages the enormous task of running her business, something stood out: she spends an hour and a half every morning in quiet time. No matter what is happening, she always finds time to be still and be quiet or learn.

This isn't a new concept. Any of those ever-popular articles with variations on the title, "The Five Things Every Successful CEO Does Each Day" includes some self-care. These conversations are happening at the leadership level, but it's important for everyone to make space for it. We've made self-care into a luxury, like it's precious and you have to get up at four in the morning to do it.

It's not that rare, but *you* have to do it. No one will smack you and make you take the time you need to rejuvenate. No one will hand you a menu of feel-goods. You have to do the self-work to discover self-care and achieve self-kindness.

Figuring out what type of self-care works for you is one of the most generous things you can do for yourself. In the discussion of the Harvard happiness study, the study's director said, "Taking care of your body is important, but tending to your relationships is a form of self-care too. That, I think, is the revelation." So maybe you're someone who works out, or someone who meditates, or maybe you spend time with a loved one or your family. I manage wellness by managing my alone time because that's what I need to be a good human. But be honest with yourself about what it is. It may not be the obvious "going out with friends!" or "watching my daughter play volleyball." We all have habits or routines that might not serve our actual needs.

What do you need to manage your mental health? Identify it, and then allow yourself to have it. This all feels kind of obvious, right? But we still don't do it.

A "Nice" Interruption

I have to take a moment to distinguish between nice and kind. To me, they are very different, or at least have very different cultural connotations, and it's important we all agree on this.

What we mean when we use the word *nice* is often masked as something else, usually something (ironically) not nice. Even the definition of *nice* is so meh that once you look at it more closely, you really start to wonder why the hell anyone would want to be nice. It means "pleasant, agreeable, satisfactory." I don't know about you, but I hope I'm described as something other than "satisfactory." The dictionary definition of *kindness* is more complex: "friendly, generous, considerate." That feels warmer and more thoughtful than nice.

Nice is playing it safe and not rocking the boat. Nice is fueled by a desire to be liked, not a desire to truly help and connect with another person. Nice is saying the easy thing and taking the path of least resistance. We play nice when we want something from someone but don't want to ask them directly. Nice is often passive-aggressive with a sugar coating: "Of *course*, I'll get that to you *right away*."

Kindness, on the other hand, is respecting others and letting go of your ego. Kindness is caring enough about people to recognize the impact we have on them. Kindness can be hard, and uncomfortable, and unknown, and uncertain. It's like love: I love my son, but if I give him everything he asks for because he wants it, I'm not doing him any favors.

It's not real love. In those moments, I need to dig deeper and think about what is truly good for him. Kindness works the same way.

We grew up believing that nice is sweet and the way we should treat people to feel good. But that's a one-dimensional truth. To do good work, we have to confront truths and dig into complex ideas—and that will necessarily include more dimensions. If your interest is in working effectively and getting to the best end results (and it should be!), that meaningful work can't occur in shallow relationships.

- Nice is superficial; kindness has depth.

- Nice is saying the safe thing; kind is doing the right thing.

- Nice centers you and your feelings; kindness centers others.

- Nice is careful; kind is thoughtful. (See "Giving Feedback" in chapter 6 for a refresher!)

Kindness in Action

Kindness is a muscle that atrophies when we ignore it. There are a million ways to do it, and a million ways it can look. Focus on substantial things over superficial things. Focus on them, not you. Acknowledge and recognize people's work.

Start smiling. Yes, I know that women get enough of that advice from asshats on the street, but ignore that—if you can—and think about how it *does* feel better to smile when you're engaging with others. If you have "resting bitch face," think about how that might affect your conversations and relationships and talk about it openly. Don't smile for the jerks (and give them a good ol' middle finger from me), but smile for the energy it creates around you.

Being Honest

Honesty is so important to mention here (in addition to the communication chapter) because we often use kindness as an excuse to avoid it: "It's not kind to tell them their idea is flawed" or "It's not nice to say no to the client." I think I've established that kindness isn't about doing the easy thing or the thing that rocks the boat the least. Kindness is doing the thing that is *for the best*. If an idea is flawed, its originator should hear about it (in a kind way). If a client or customer is making an undoable ask, then they should learn about that (in a kind way). Kindness is in the delivery, not the message itself.

We all want honesty from others. When our zipper is down, when there's spinach in our teeth, when our spreadsheet has an error, when our presentation needs more practice, when our service could be improved— as humans, we need this. Even when it's hard, we are usually grateful when someone makes an effort to be honest with us because it's a relief. It's a chance to grow. It's easier than bullshit, which the world is too full of.

Honesty is kindness because it allows us to grow, improve, and thrive. It also means that you're paying attention and want to contribute to the work and people around you. At Clockwork, our first value is *We tell the truth and keep our promises.* Both clients and colleagues expect me to be 100 percent transparent and honest with them at all times, and I expect the same from them. That means being honest about bad news, inconvenient needs, and uncomfortable truths. We're also honest when we're appreciative, satisfied, and impressed (yes, sometimes the positive stuff is as hard to say!).

I work in the service space, and one of the hardest things to fight when it comes to honesty is the "customer is always right" mentality. If you're not in the service space, replace "customer" with "boss" or "loudest person in the room." It could be the executive who claims a bright idea that you see holes in, or a boss who says you should be able to absorb your previous colleague's tasks now that he quit.

Although customers (and indeed, most people) never want to hear that they're wrong, I learned early on that you get yourself in much more trouble if you don't tell the truth about capabilities, expectations, and issues. If I say, "I can do that," and I can't, it won't start our relationship off on the right foot. And I know that, so it's not kind. If we go back to the definition of *kind*—generous and considerate—we can see how saying yes when you know it's impossible is not kind. But when I look carefully at what we *can* do to help that client and offer it, I am displaying goodwill and generosity, and showing them that I want to do what I can. I have made a career out of crushing unrealistic dreams—but then working to build attainable ones. That's the simple recipe: honestly represent the issues and then work to be solution-focused. If being honest requires saying no, offer an alternative. To the executive with the not-thought-through idea, don't lead with what's wrong: lead with "yes, and" and append some ideas that will help make it better. To the boss who is having you do double the work, offer a compromise or prepare a plan that proposes a better solution *for the business.*

An environment of honesty builds a deep level of trust, security, and collaboration. Clockwork employees and clients relish our open communication because straightforwardness, accessibility, and transparency replace shame, guilt, and baggage (and the passive-aggression that fuel them!). Honesty makes people feel like you have their back.

Being honest like a Boss means integrating all the attributes we've talked about into how you show up in the conversation: accepting accountability for telling it, fearing less when you have to do it, embracing the human side of your message as you're doing it, and engaging respectfully and empathetically throughout. Honesty is key to finding power and fulfillment.

Not every company or leader is ready for honesty. It can fail when a team or company values comfort and consensus over . . . well, anything more productive. It can fail when a leader isn't comfortable hearing truths and working together on solutions. A friend shared the following story about her experience in a Minnesota company: "I was in a large company with a passive-aggressive boss who wouldn't let any conflict occur, even in decision-making or brainstorming. At one point, we were in a seminar at the office during which a 'business etiquette' expert came in to lecture about appropriate 'business casual' attire for men and women. This lecturer said that women did not look professional without lipstick. I asked her if that was sexist, and she said no, it was just proper etiquette and women looked better with lipstick. I was incredulous, and then I got written up for interrupting the lecturer."

Honesty in an environment like that can be hard because there are negative consequences for honest actions. That happens, I know. But incremental progress is still progress. If you let the idea of never being able to improve everything get in the way of improving anything, you'll feel defeated all the time. Start with honesty about the smallest things, and you might be able to penetrate the fiction—and attitudes—that dishonesty creates.

Ditching the Cutthroat Competition

Dominant culture defines professionalism as cutthroat and competitive. Maybe it's a leftover understanding from wartime eras, when survival required fighting to the death, but its effects are real: we sabotage others, we place blame, we don't share credit or information. You don't have to be on the trading-room floor or work in a high-powered law office to experience aspects of cutthroat culture. It's built into bonus structures, promotion cycles, and individual performance ratings.

Recently, a colleague told me a story about a close friend who landed a job at a startup. When she was interviewing and vetting the company, the work culture seemed amazing. The website and team said all the right things. The questions she asked in her interviews didn't throw people off and made her feel confident about the workplace. About six months after she took the job, she was feeling really crappy. Over her short time there, she watched people sabotage their peers and purposefully derail projects. Rather than quit immediately, she went to her boss to talk through her concerns. His response was telling: "Yeah, you just have to play the game." The game. Her career and all those employees' feelings and ideas are just a game in a culture like that.

In a cutthroat workplace, it's me over all else. That's an old-school way of thinking. The article "8 Ways Cutthroat Work Cultures Suck the Life Out of You,"[51] shares the effects of this particular kind of work culture:

- It overworks people.

- There's no empathy.

- It doesn't recognize contributions or reward good work.

- There's no socializing and no fun.

- It makes a lot of pointless rules.

- People don't help each other out.

- It doesn't let people pursue their passions.

- Bosses don't listen.

Cutthroat culture, as painted in these points, is the opposite of what most people want to experience at work. And it's the opposite of what nearly every modern study recommends for productivity at work (and what I've been talking about now for the last hundred-plus pages). I think we all know this from personal experience. Even if we've never

---

51 Travis Bradberry, "8 Ways Cutthroat Work Cultures Suck the Life Out of You," *Entrepreneur*, November 1, 2016, https://www.entrepreneur.com/article/284385.

been in that dramatic of a cutthroat environment, we've all been through competition that didn't feel good.

Cutthroat doesn't work for work *now*. If you search for skills that employers are actually looking for in employees, the most popular include qualities that are impossible to grow in a cutthroat environment, things like honesty, collaboration, and communication and people skills. Cutthroat cultures kill qualities like those; they leave no room for anything else.

I think we're slowly starting to realize that not everyone works in the same way—and there aren't inherently good or bad ways. That is why we have to make space for *all* ways. Competition favors the people who fight, not the ones who have good ideas. It favors the people who want to fight, not those who want to do the best work. I am loud, but I am not competitive—I relate to the tortoise, not the hare, in the classic fable. I built my business and my path to success on community over competition in part because I would not have succeeded through competition. But I have good ideas. And if that's true of me, it stands to be true of others.

Leadership, management, and traditional work culture might plant the seeds of competition at work, but people perpetuate it. We learned this mentality in school, in popular representations of work, and probably in our own work histories. And we carry it with us. I see people come into Clockwork with this ingrained in them, not necessarily because they are naturally competitive but because it's the way they learned to work. They come in wanting to be the best, the smartest, the fastest, the most anything.

I work hard to nix that attitude when I see it, both directly and indirectly. I have conversations with people about their competitive behaviors and try to get them to see how it's not productive in a culture driven by teamwork. You can't share credit and ideas if your internal motivation is winning or outpacing your colleagues. I demonstrate that and also point to how we operate differently. We reward people for behaviors we want to cultivate and hope that positive reinforcement underscores our commitment to working in a different way.

Competition has a necessary structure: us versus them, or me versus everything. If there is a sense of "them" to anything you're working on, it will achieve less than its potential. If you have a "them," you have created an Other, and othering omits empathy, inclusivity, and authentic collaboration. The most dangerous outcome could be excluding customers. Any air of an us-versus-them attitude can spoil a lot more than a single team on the fourth floor. It can pervade every part of your personal and business experience, and that's a risk no company wants to take.

Untangling the cutthroat from our DNA doesn't mean our work cultures will be or should be "gold star for everyone" environments. The opposite of cutthroat isn't cuddly. It's welcoming and accountable.

Seeing People

Remember Bad Boss? He sucked, big time. But the moment I knew I would never go back to work for him, I also knew how I was going to treat the people I work with: I would value humans simply for being human. We often value people for what they can do, what they bring to the table, or what we can get from them. But if we step back and value them for *being there*, we can see them for who they are and the ideas they have. And with this approach, we can build more welcoming, inclusive spaces.

Sometime in the late 1990s I was interviewed by a magazine, and we talked about all the new internet technologies taking the business world by storm. The interviewer asked me, in the middle of the conversation, what my legacy would be. I paused for a minute and then said something like, "Well, it won't be websites. I think I want my legacy to be about new ways of working. How the internet has powered new behaviors and opportunities and new accountabilities. And it's ushering in new work cultures that require independence and curiosity and flexibility and power."

The internet forced so much of the change we need at work. It enabled us to work from *anywhere* in so many industries. But it won't fix our human resistance to change. It won't fix our bad habits. And it doesn't mean we'll never have to work with people. We still have to do the work. We still have to look inside and examine why we sabotage ourselves and each other. I think I always knew this. I always expected that the internet might make the business systems easier, but people are still hard. Until we do the analog work, digital transformations don't guarantee success.

Inclusivity is a conversation in business right now because we are underperforming without it. As a developed country, we are less than we could be if we included different perspectives in our work. Our products would be more valuable if we included more people in our processes and workplaces. Our audiences and economy would be bigger.

For so much of our history, certain people thought they literally had more value than others. Centuries of behaviors and beliefs are still there, and we have a lot to do to rid our systems of them. We have to retrain our brains and ourselves to encode something new into our work DNA.

Inclusivity is about creating a sense of belonging. Humans have a universal desire to belong. They thrive in environments in which they do. Psychological safety and kindness are the surest and fastest ways to generate that feeling around you. When we are unkind, we are not creating a sense of belonging. We have to feel like we belong in all parts of our lives.

As we've seen in the perpetuation of workplaces that look the same way—white, middle-to-upper class, educated, cisgender, and straight—humans tend to want to work with people like them. It feels like a good fit! But we have to start to want to work with people who *aren't* like us. We have to create work cultures that intentionally welcome a variety of people, where a cultural fit is about values and principles, not demographics.

Consciously contributing to belonging in the workplace might be the biggest challenge in this book because it requires the ultimate un-centering of ourselves. It asks us to think about how to activate others and requires us to make more room at the proverbial table. But if we do this, we can get better. Together.

Inclusivity is a complex and sensitive topic, but on a human scale, we can accomplish a lot through small, thoughtful actions.[52] It's recognizing

---

52 There are entire books, studies, and programs devoted to the importance of inclusivity and diversity, how to plan for it, and how to train people around it. This book is not that. This book is about you. But it wouldn't be honest, helpful, or responsible to not acknowledge the critical importance of inclusion and your role in it.

and appreciating differences—all differences, including race, physical ability, age, mental health, and educational background. It's opening yourself up to personal connection and inviting others to do the same by asking simple questions about their families, their pastimes, and their religious or spiritual beliefs. Some of those things might feel weird to talk about at work, but the workplace assumption that people celebrate Christmas is just us taking religion for granted. It's learning how to be an ally to the people around you and encourage everyone around you to do so as well. Think of what makes you feel welcomed, and do that.

Most of us wait for our bosses to say, "You're doing a good job!" to feel like we're doing a good job. We wait to be acknowledged to feel like we contributed. But we are inherently valuable because we're human, and *we have the power to value others.*

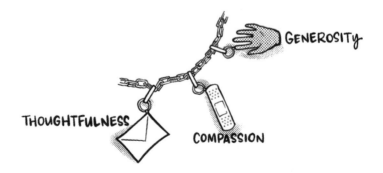

Practicing Generosity

In our personal relationships, we probably think good communication, great chemistry, or shared values are the key to long-lasting love. That is certainly what many magazines would have us believe. But psychologist John Gottman has done several studies showing that it is none of that. Healthy relationships are grounded in kindness and generosity. We've already defined kindness, so let's look a little closer at the word *generous*. We often associate it with monetary or tangible items, but it's also inclusive of spending more time and attention than necessary. Being generous can look like giving people the benefit of the doubt or assuming the best (or at least not the worst). Generosity can be offering to help or just being there to support a peer going through a difficult time at work.

In an *Atlantic* article that dives into the study I mention above, the author notes, "One way to practice kindness is by being generous about your partner's intentions." It continues,

> Say a wife is running late to dinner (again), and the husband assumes that she doesn't value him enough to show up to their date on time after he took the trouble to make a reservation and leave work early so that they could spend a romantic evening together. But it turns out that the wife was running late because she stopped by a store to pick him up a gift for their special night out. Imagine her joining him for dinner, excited to deliver her gift, only to realize that

he's in a sour mood because he misinterpreted what was motivating her behavior.

And now here is the part to remember: "The ability to interpret your partner's actions and intentions charitably can soften the sharp edge of conflict."[53]

Replace *partner* with *colleague,* and suddenly we've all been in a situation like that. Maybe recently a colleague has been late to nearly every meeting or has been canceling them altogether. The knee-jerk reaction is to be irritated. You might even be tempted to practice that comfortable habit of passive-aggression and shut down a bit to punish them. The kind way to handle the situation is to say how it makes you feel: "It's hard for me when you're late because I feel like I'm wasting time since I can't jump into new tasks while I'm waiting." And then ask if there is anything you can do to help. We've all had days where we barely have time to go to the bathroom between meetings. Perhaps a generous, kind, and equitable solution is simply scheduling meetings for thirty-five minutes after the hour instead of thirty, when their prior meeting ends. Everyone wins! But only if you're generous in the first place.

If we continue thinking about work relationships like we do our

---

53 Emily Esfahani Smith, "Masters of Love," *The Atlantic,* June 12, 2014, https://www. theatlantic.com/health/archive/2014/06/happily-ever-after/372573/.

personal ones, this point from the *Atlantic* article should drive home the role of kindness and generosity: "There are many reasons why relationships fail, but if you look at what drives the deterioration of many relationships, it's often a breakdown of kindness."

In correlated research, the Gottman Institute articulated the Four Horsemen of relationships: criticism, contempt, defensiveness, and stonewalling.[54] These things are counterproductive to effective relationships. Criticism is attacks on the person or their personal qualities in judgmental terms versus critiquing the work or giving feedback on how something impacted you. Contempt is basically aggression with a side of moral superiority; it includes things like belittling, eye-rolling, and dismissing another person. Defensiveness is making excuses or placing blame rather than participating in self-reflection. And stonewalling is

---

54 Ellie Lisitsa, "The Four Horsemen: Criticism, Contempt, Defensiveness, and Stonewalling," Gottman Institute, April 23, 2013, https://www.gottman.com/blog/the-four-horsemen-recognizing-criticism-contempt-defensiveness-and-stonewalling/.

just shutting down and withdrawing from an interaction or conversation altogether. Again, applying this idea to work relationships and scenarios is pretty easy. We see these human-but-unhelpful behaviors every day at work—and probably in *ourselves.*

What to do? Go back to kindness and generosity. Gottman has helpful antidotes to these unkind actions.[55] I've reframed his examples with work themes.

If you're feeling critical, express a positive need or frame up your message in the first person rather than firing away with *You always . . .* Say, "I'd love to take on some of the higher-profile projects or help you with them" rather than "You always take the big projects, you're such an attention hog."

If you're feeling contempt, first own it and be kind to yourself despite your less-than-helpful reaction. Then try to understand or identify with the other person in how you express yourself. "I know you're under some stress right now, but it's important for our reputation that our work is top-notch. I'm happy to help you," rather than, "Your work is always so sloppy, I'll just have to redo it . . . *again."*

If you're feeling defensive, find a way to take responsibility or even acknowledge the situation without blaming. "Yes, this did not go as well

---

55 Ellie Lisitsa, "The Four Horsemen: The Antidotes," Gottman Institute, April 26, 2013, https://www.gottman.com/blog/the-four-horsemen-the-antidotes/.

as I wanted or as well as it could have," instead of, "It's not my fault the team dragged their feet on it."

If you're stonewalling and shutting down during a conversation, find a way to fight it. It could be asking for a short break to gather your thoughts or practice what you'd like to say so you feel prepared for the conversation.

If you're thinking, "Jeez, this is so much psychology!" you're right. Because psychology is about human behavior, and finding your power and happiness at work essentially comes down to understanding humans. The rest—your expertise and knowledge and information—is table stakes. The rest is how to feel empowered and succeed.

Feeling productive and collaborative feels good. I truly believe that we all *want* to do good work. We all want to come home after a workday feeling like we contributed. Healthy and functional relationships at work are so important in accomplishing that.

Going Back to Basics

Kindness sounds simple or even plain. And though it is frequently both simple and plain, it is often not easy. Kindness can be confusing, daunting, and uncomfortable. When it's those things, selfishness will be the fastest, easiest option. Resist it!

Attending to your own comfort at your colleagues' expense doesn't just damage their work experience; it fractures the organization as a whole. It's a cycle: you reduce the health of the culture with selfishness, which creates friction, which makes people more uncomfortable, which creates more opportunities for you to react with selfishness. Rinse and repeat.

So get personal. Not intimate or inappropriate—just demonstrate that you register someone's individual needs.

- Check in—on a project, or on how they're doing.

- Have a conversation rather than sending an email.

- Shine a light on someone's achievements, creativity, energy, curiosity, or joy, or how well they connect with others.

- Offer to go over that thing you made or the document you wrote.

- Take clients and colleagues out to coffee to see how they feel about a project. Ask what's frustrating and what's rewarding.

- Offer help or extend your expertise.

- Cover for someone so they can see their kid's basketball

game at 4:00 p.m. (why, oh why, do kids' sports do this to us?!).

I had a mentor who said, "Problems are opportunities." I always appreciated this positive spin. I try to see every problem as a way to grow, improve, or learn. Bosses not only believe this, they live it. They fill gaps, and that includes emotional gaps, not just business gaps.

If you get nothing else from this book, remember that how work feels is on *you*. You're accountable. We want to blame leadership and management. It's all their fault, right? They do the hiring, they make the decisions, and they write the rules. That's mostly true, but your actions make up the culture.

Each of us has the ability to change how work feels for us and others around us. Think of the change we could make by simply not taking part in watercooler venting. That contagion might not change the whole company, but it can change your shift or your day or your week. It can change your own sense of happiness, and that, in turn, can change other humans around you. Imagine giving the gift of a little more joy to someone else. When you show up in a positive, kind way, you are actually changing the world.

So just be fucking kind. You'll live longer! And happier! Like a Boss.

Work Like a Boss Takeaways

1. Kindness requires intention and deliberate behavior—it's a muscle that atrophies when we don't use it enough. Get thoughtful.
2. Work relationships can be the source of peril or promise; treat them as seriously, emotionally, and strategically as you do your personal relationships.
3. Kindness is simple but not easy. Give your time, effort, energy, and heart to what you're doing and the people around you.

Chapter Eight

THE SECRET

- Accountability is the key to any change at work. *You* must be the instigator.

- Fear is a jerk and ruins us. Fearing less can help you shake off paralysis and start moving in an intentional direction.

- Work and people are messy. They are unpredictable and constantly changing, and that's just how it's going to be. Your power comes in accepting and embracing that.

- More communication is always better. Practice openness, get comfortable with discomfort, and read the room to find power in effective, clear communication.

- Exhibiting kindness can make work—and you—more joyful.

Over the course of our lifetime, we will spend thirteen-plus years of our lives working. By comparison, we will spend 328 days socializing with people we care about. It's a shame to think about spending that kind of time doing something we don't care about and are not invested in. It's a shame not to think about work, and our work relationships, with the same dedication we bring to our personal lives.

If we don't change how we approach work, we will be miserable. If we don't change how we invest ourselves at work, we will be miserable. And who wants to spend more than thirteen *years* being miserable? Who actually *wants* to not enjoy the people they have to interact, share space, and collaborate with day in and day out? What is the point of not trying to do meaningful work with people who matter to you?

We read or see stories all the time about people doing amazing things at work. Doctors save lives, teachers change lives, and artists make our lives more creative. But most jobs aren't like that. Most of us aren't Nobel Prize winners doing anything terribly noteworthy. I know I'm not. But everyone who works is contributing something necessary: performing a service, building a product, helping an organization succeed. That is all necessary. *You* are necessary.

We are all more necessary than we're aware. Your perspective, diligence, desire, and interest shape whatever you're doing. And all that—no matter your job—makes a difference. The nurse I have matters to me. If she cares and is invested, if she feels valued and supported, and if she is seen and appreciated, she could save my life.

There is no point in spending our time at work if we can't enjoy parts of it or be proud of what we do. I have a friend who worked at a bagel shop twenty years ago when she was a teenager. She is still proud of her sandwich-making skills and feels genuine joy in what she made for customers there. The job certainly didn't feel important in the big scheme of things, and she didn't intend to pursue a career in the food industry, but that didn't stop her from finding something in it that she could dedicate her energy to. She had to do all the crap work too—wash dishes, take out garbage, and sweep up after guests—but she balanced that "meh" with the art of making perfectly proportioned sandwiches and serving them to people who enjoyed them.

We need to find ways to dig in and do our best at work. And our best isn't about perfection. Our best is our energy, how we treat people, and the kindness, courage, and bravery we find within ourselves every day. It's taking risks and trying something new, even when it's hard. It's encouraging and supporting the people around us to help them. It's wanting to grow for the sake of growing.

Our best is not stagnating. Our best is not punching in and punching out. Our best isn't putting a butt in a seat.

Our best is really living at work. Our best isn't easy, but it's necessary and requires intention.

What's the secret to doing this every day? There is no secret. I wish it

were as simple as "If you think it, you will manifest it," but intention and thoughtfulness, hard work, improvement, evolution, and contribution all take energy. Effort and practice are as important as the desire to be our best. It requires personal accountability. We have to *decide* to show up every day. Your power and joy manifest not in a particular outcome, but in *caring* about an outcome.

If we don't do some of these things every day, what are we spending all our time doing? Nothing. We're creating our own misery.

But we can create our own joy. In my talks, I always say that happiness is made from small moments strung together into a larger story. We think happiness comes in big packages: a huge wedding, a lake house, a fancy car, a perfect body. But I think happiness comes in small moments, like taking your dog for a walk in fresh snow, reading a book with your kid, having a glass of wine with a dear friend, making that perfect cup of coffee. These moments, when you feel them and appreciate them, create happiness *right now*. The same is true for work. We can believe happiness comes with getting that promotion, beating out the other company for the client's business, getting a big bonus, or being a boss, but that's shortsighted. Taking pride in small moments at work brings us joy at work—when you solve a problem you hadn't solved before, build a connection with someone new, or fail but learn from it. If we readjust our scope from macro to micro and do things *right now* that make an impact on us, the people around us, and our organizations, we can be happy at work.

If you want to work like a Boss, take ownership. Believe that the organization, its reputation, its product, and its revenue are yours. Because they are. Step up and own it. Show up like you own the place every day. Hold yourself accountable for that.

As a country, we have to do all of this now. The economy and technology are moving so quickly that we don't have time to wait. The most valuable people inside any and every organization are the ones I've described here.

To work like a Boss:

- Be optimistic

- Take initiative

- Try, and keep trying

- Be kind

- See opportunities instead of problems

- Be solution-focused

- Bring good energy

- Say yes and jump into something new

- Offer your best ideas and share credit

- Show empathy and compassion for colleagues

- Create space that encourages creativity

- Bring out the best in others

- Embrace differences and diversity

- Contribute to a sense of belonging

- Feel a personal responsibility for the organization

- Take accountability for the culture

It doesn't matter where people fall within the hierarchy of a company: this is what's needed from everybody if the organization is to succeed. It's also what our country needs if we want to remain relevant and a leader in the global marketplace. That's how important your attitude at work is: our nation needs innovation and new ideas to stay ahead. If every single person felt that urgency and relevance on an individual scale, think of the things we could achieve.

You can blame everybody else for the lack of opportunities you've experienced, but you play a part in it. Have you networked your ass off?

Did you ask at every turn for the thing you wanted and demonstrate that you could do it? Have you taken 100 percent initiative at every role and job you've held? You can blame your family, the leaders of your workplace, or your manager for your failure to feel good about your work, but it's not their responsibility. It is yours.

The patriarchy and white supremacy hold people back. I can't fix that with one book, but you and I and all of us can take small steps to make that reality less true and eventually untrue. If every person works like a Boss, we can make more diverse workplaces. If every person applies the values and beliefs they hold in their personal lives to their work lives, we can build more inclusive work cultures.

I called this book *Work Like a Boss* because the best bosses do these things. If they don't, they fail. If they don't encourage great work from the people around them or acknowledge good ideas wherever they come from, they will have a bad team. If they are negative and complain all the time, no one will want to follow them. No one wants to work *for* or *with* a leader with that attitude.

In the introduction, I talked about the importance of thinkers, feelers, and doers. Bosses *do*. They reflect the entrepreneurial spirit. The root of the word *entrepreneur* is *entreprendre*, which is derived from Old French and means "to undertake." The only real difference between an entrepreneur and everyone else is that they *do*: they undertake, they take on, they tackle whatever it is that needs undertaking. We can take that way of being and apply it to any job or position inside of any organization. We can be "intrapreneurs"—the people inside of an organization who embrace an entrepreneurial attitude and attributes. In business, stagnation is death. Look no further than Blockbuster or failing department stores for evidence of that. The same is true of individuals. If you want to stay in that shitty job, if you want to wallow in your shitty attitude, then do it. But the rest of us can't afford that, and you'll soon find that it limits your opportunities as well as your happiness.

We need to be better. We need to own our shit, fix our shit, be nice, and plow through negativity at all costs. Use your voice—strategically and thoughtfully. Use your energy—positively and purposefully. Use your ideas—fearlessly and compassionately. Do all that even when you're terrified.

Regardless of where you work—in a large corporation, in a small organization, or at something other than an office—there is a work culture, and you are responsible for it. What do you want from that culture? Create it.

There will be challenges and setbacks, but there is no reward for

doing easy stuff. If you are going to devote thirteen years and more to work, what is the point in not showing up as your whole self, welcoming others, and being proud of what you do?

Nothing I've said here is a roadmap or an all-encompassing directive. Past generations worked, bought a house, retired, and died on schedule, but work doesn't come with checklists or stage-by-stage guides anymore. The whole landscape is different now, but you've got this! Do some of these things when you can. Choose incremental growth. Any amount of growth is a step in the right direction. We owe it to ourselves to change the perceptions of work that were defined a century ago, like the powerlessness that most people feel if they aren't the boss. We are not powerless or helpless. We might not be the boss, but we are valuable and we can value other people.

We *can* be part of change and success. We *can* feel good about going to work. It's not on anyone else to make that a reality. It's not on anyone else to fix *it* or *us*. It is on us—on *you*. The solution isn't in an app or a to-do list; the decision to do it, more than anything, is the secret.

If you change yourself first, you will feel better. You will start to show up at work differently and shape the culture around you differently. And that is working like a Boss.

ACKNOWLEDGMENTS

There's a moment in one of my talks in which I remind audiences that nothing good ever happens because of just one person. I emphasize that point dramatically and use Steve Jobs as an example. We hold him up as a visionary genius responsible for one of the most successful companies in the world. And then I talk about the many many humans holding Steve and his vision and Apple up always. This is absolutely true in all things: Nothing good ever happens because of just one person. I can point to critical collaborators, supporters, mentors, friends, and cheerleaders throughout my entire career. And this book is no different. I have a huge team of coaches, friends, colleagues, coworkers, business partners, influencers, mentors, readers, advisors, twitter friends, and editors who made this book happen, whether they were aware of their roles or not.

Here are just some of the people who were a part of the process.

I could not even function if not for Lyz Nagan. Lyz is my partner in words and the person who makes sense of most of my crazy ideas. I feel really fortunate to call Lyz a collaborator and a friend. And I'm so grateful she helped me make my dream of this book come true.

My pals and business partners: Chuck Hermes, Mike Koppelman, and Kurt Koppelman. I've often said I'm more married to them than to my spouse. And if I have to be married to men, these are some damn good ones. I'm grateful.

I have huge gratitude for Dara Beevas. She has been an inspiration from the moment I met her and she has been unwavering in her desire to support me making this book. Dara was a coach, a counselor, an editor, a contributor, a friend, and a therapist in this process. She's so good at what she does: I always felt cared for and heard.

Thanks to Chloe Radcliffe who helped a pile of ideas take shape and truly become something worth seeing through to the end. I don't think she has any idea how valuable her guidance was in this process.

I have the best leadership team on the planet. Without them, there is no book. I'm proud to work with them and learn from them all the time. Jenny Holman, Vince Cabansag, Micah Spieler, Dean Huff, and Scott Jackson: thank you for being truly accountable and showing up fueled by challenge every single day.

Having Mahtab Rezai as a friend was gift enough. But getting to call her a coworker and collaborator has been a delight. I am so inspired by her courage, vision, and thoughtfulness in everything she does. She read the book and got so excited about it, and that was the final push I really needed.

I have admired Lisa Troutman's work from across rooms and

auditoriums for ages. Getting to write a book made whole by her illustrations is a huge honor. I can't even express how excited I am by the illustrations in this book and how perfectly they fit into every chapter. My appreciation for her contribution is enormous. Plus, I now have a drawing of me standing in—and owning—my shit. If that's not a great reminder to walk the walk I don't know what is.

Meghan McInerny has had such an impact on my professional life. Her influence is all over these pages. Together, we have tackled every challenge I talk about in this book, and I have come out on the other side with more trust, gratitude, and appreciation for her. She's a process genius, a calming force in the midst of chaos, a born leader, and a great friend.

I need to thank every single past, present, and future Clockworker. Clockwork isn't a thing. It's people. And the people I've had the privilege of working with over the years have been some of the very best. They've taught me my most valuable life lessons.

Thank you to my dear friends and chosen family formed at Chi-Chi's in City Center (one way or another). That group of humans taught me some of the most important, most formative lessons of my life, and, at the time, I had no idea. Todd Jones, Stephen Reed, Joe Konizeski, Andy Ogg, Jane Greathouse: I love you like siblings forever. Thanks, Chi-Chi's.

Sue Remes has huge enthusiasm and encouragement for literally everything I do, and I cherish that. Knowing that such a great person is always on my team feels amazing. I am so grateful for our friendship.

If I didn't have Davis Senseman to call or text in the middle of all the frustrating things, I would be a ball of nerves. I call Davis "the fixer" for a number of reasons, but mostly because they are the best damn business and life advisor on the planet. And they are so humble that they probably don't even know how grateful I am. But maybe now they do.

I have huge gratitude for the women leaders and mentors from my WPO groups: Minnesota Chapter 4 and Platinum 6. This collection of business executives are some of the most brilliant, driven, fierce women I know. Big thanks to Sue Hawkes, who made certain I came to the second meeting. And changed my life.

My dear friend Amy Zaroff has more energy and chutzpah than just about anybody on the planet. And she channeled a good chunk of that my way and pushed for this book.

Thank you to Gino Wickman, Casey Boys, Nora McInerny, and Kai Rysdall for saying yes without hesitation.

Thank you to Nathan Tylutki for reading every word. And then reading them again. Probably from a bathtub somewhere.

I have deep gratitude for my past and present Family Equality family.

The chance to collaborate and lead with all of you has informed parts of my life and this book in enormous ways.

I'm grateful to the momsquad—my crazy little group of friends that came together because of our kids' school. Jennifer Bawcom, Emily Knox, Maggie Johnson, Lauren Ferrera, Radhika Naidu Thompson, and Sarabeth Scott: your excitement and encouragement every time I mentioned this book were more helpful than you know.

Avery Swartz was such a huge help in her willingness to share literally everything she knows about everything without pause. And she knows A LOT. So many thank yous for the conversations and emails.

No one has ever been such a champion for me as Julie Allinson is. I am humbled by her willingness to mentor and advise and push and cajole and be so direct and honest and unapologetically supportive. Her friendship means the world to me.

Having a writer review my writing was terrifying, but Michael Opperman was kind and generous with his feedback. I am in awe of his way with words. And I am grateful that he shared some of them with me and made time to validate this little book.

I can't thank my social media community enough. Every single person who sent in a story or shared experiences from their own workplaces or work histories helped me in this process. Though I didn't end up using specific accounts in the way I thought I would, I still reference those stories and the behaviors throughout the book.

Thank you to my nurse friends. Though you shall remain nameless, that conversation we had over that dinner that one night in the summer was exactly the validation I needed to believe this book could be for any profession. Your willingness to share your experiences was humbling.

The Twin Cities business community is an amazingly safe haven for someone like me. I have felt valuable support from MSP for the past twenty-five years. I can't imagine doing this work anywhere else.

To City of Lakes Waldorf School: I have learned so much alongside my son. What a gift.

And finally, my family; my families.

I'm grateful to my FOO (Family Of Origin). Our FOOs shape us in ways that define our futures and mine made me a big mouth. I wouldn't be who I am without my mom, dad, and sister: Barbara and Bill Lyons and Kat Lyons. Thank you for still putting up with me.

I have a great appreciation for the Niewald family for accepting me and making me a part of this big, boisterous, loud, loving family. Especially Dolores, who never batted an eye. She just opened her arms.

And lastly, all things are possible and worthwhile because of my little family at home. Laura Niewald and Merrick Lyons: I love our little life together. Always.

ABOUT THE AUTHOR

Nancy Lyons is a national speaker and co-founder/CEO of Clockwork, an award-winning digital agency in Minneapolis, Minnesota. As a leader in the technology industry for more than twenty-five years, she has developed and proven her people-first business strategy and has demonstrated the impact of work culture on work performance. Her work with Fortune 1000 businesses, her roles on boards of directors, and her involvement in politics have honed her ability to tell hard truths, connect with people, and learn from real-world experiences. She is candid, funny, and always says what everyone else in the room is afraid to say.

Schedule Nancy to speak at your next event!

Nancy is an energetic speaker who tailors every talk for the audience at hand. With a commanding, candid, and entertaining presentation style, she always makes people think differently about work and life. Whether you have a group of 10,000 or 10, Nancy will add value and inspire curiosity.

Talk titles have included:

- "Work Like a Boss: Five Steps to Finding (and Using) Your Power at Work"

- "Bring Your (Inner) Boss to Post-Pandemic Work: How to Lead in This New Environment"

- "Cultivating a Human-centered work culture: How Every Person Contributes to How Work Feels"

- "Being an Employee, Thinking Like a CEO: Core Attributes to Bring to Every Job"

Get more information and connect at www.nancylyons.com.